RACE AGAINST TIME

All persons born or naturalized in the United States, and subject to the jurisdiction thereof, are citizens of the United States and of the State wherein they reside. No State shall make or enforce any law which shall abridge the privileges or immunities of citizens of the United States; nor shall any State deprive any person of life, liberty, or property, without due process of law; nor deny to any person within its jurisdiction the equal protection of the laws."

—US CONSTITUTION
Fourteenth Amendment,
Section I

THE UNTOLD STORY OF SCIPIO JONES AND
THE BATTLE TO SAVE TWELVE INNOCENT MEN

RACE AGAINST TIME

SANDRA NEIL WALLACE
& RICH WALLACE

CALKINS CREEK
AN IMPRINT OF BOYDS MILLS & KANE
New York

IN MEMORY OF **Scopio A. Jones**,

FOR UPHOLDING JUSTICE WITH EVERY BREATH

Calkins Creek
An imprint of Boyds Mills & Kane, a division of Astra Publishing House
calkinscreekbooks.com
Printed in China

33614082300202

ISBN: 978-1-62979-816-5 (hc)
978-1-63592-373-5 (ebook)
Library of Congress Control Number: 2020934634

First edition
10 9 8 7 6 5 4 3 2 1

Designed by Red Herring Design
The text is set in Goudy Oldstyle, Knockout, and Eveleth.

CONTENTS

Christmas Eve, 1924
Little Rock, Arkansas

Drenched from fever, Scipio Jones struggled to find the strength to walk the five miserable miles to the governor's mansion.

Scipio had run out of fuel to heat his home, and the winter streets of Little Rock were even colder than his house. But heat didn't matter now. Words did. He'd have to find the words to pierce through the evil veil of racism shrouding the governor's mind. And if he failed? Innocent men would die, executed by electric chair, with all hope gone and the blood-soaked village of Hoop Spur, Arkansas, seeping with stories soon forgotten.

Scipio reached for his hat and cane and faced the wind. "This is a life and death struggle with us . . . we are not going to surrender."

This is the story of Scipio Jones and the twelve innocent men he defended. It's the story of a man who ignited the civil rights movement long before Dr. Martin Luther King Jr. and Rosa Parks.

corporated Union

Vhom It May Concern:

....

stoffice ....

olor .... is a member of

The Progressive Farmers & Household Union of America

Any favor extended to him or her in law or custom will be highly appreciated by us.

President, Winchester, Ark.

Gen. Atty., Little Rock, Ark.

Councilor, Winchester, Ark.

Headquarters, Washington, D. C.

Arkansas sharecroppers knew the value of their crops. Many joined the Progressive Farmers & Household Union of America to try to ensure the payment they deserved.

FIVE YEARS EARLIER

Tuesday, September 30, 1919
Hoop Spur, Arkansas

O n a moonless night, Ed Ware drove along the dirt road to church, noticing an unusual chill in the air. It felt too cold for the flatlands of the Arkansas Delta, even if it was a few hours before October. Dew collected like spiderwebs across the alfalfa thickets outside the tiny wooden building in the village of Hoop Spur—a church you would only know if you were a sharecropper and taxi driver like Ed, working the land around nearby Elaine—a town barely six months old.

It would be difficult staying awake on the church's wooden benches after working the cotton fields from sunup to sundown on land rented from white owners who, refusing to sign contracts, couldn't be trusted when paying for harvests. Even the Hoop Spur church was owned by a white merchant. Still, it was a place to show respect and be respected—a place to talk freely about the frustrations of being treated as second-class citizens.

On this Tuesday night, Ed Ware and the 200 men, women, and children entering the candlelit church knew that once their soulful voices finished singing faithful hymns, the union meeting that followed could be dangerous. Standing up for themselves always was. Yet the Great War—that's what Ed and all Americans called World War One—had changed a lot of things. Many sharecroppers fought bravely in Europe, defending the rights that they didn't have at home. When they returned, the men spoke of how they'd felt safer in the trenches than in Arkansas.

Frank Moore, the sharecropper Ed most admired at the union meeting, had enlisted. He'd been stationed at Camp Pike, where the army base was segregated. Frank had sacrificed his crops to serve his country, and had been honorably discharged when the Great War ended less than a year earlier.

Now, cotton prices were skyrocketing, but the only people benefiting from the boom were white landowners, who managed to keep Black farmers in debt by claiming that the sharecroppers never earned enough to cover the cost of their rent or supplies.

It was high time for sharecroppers to organize a union to guarantee fair prices for their harvests. But just that week, Ed Ware had been warned there would be trouble if he refused to sell his cotton for the price set by the white merchants in Elaine, and that joining a union would have serious consequences. Ed stood his ground. He hired the well-known Little Rock law firm, Bratton and Casey, to negotiate the best price for his

African American soldiers served proudly in World War One, including these men of the 369th Infantry Regiment. They returned home demanding to be treated fairly.

cotton. He'd cultivated a bumper crop and refused to sell at rock-bottom prices.

But ignoring the threats would be foolish. All summer throughout the country, Black people had faced deadly retaliation for peacefully standing up for their rights. Much blood had been shed in a season that became known as Red Summer. That's why it was no surprise when Ed walked past armed guards—some of them his friends—to get inside the church for the meeting. They'd been hired by the Progressive Farmers & Household Union, which had met in the Hoop Spur church a few times already.

Some of the farmers brought their rifles for protection and

set them in a corner. As secretary of the union, all Ed had was a pencil and a notebook, and he got to work recording dues for the union, ignoring the pain in his swollen fingers from decades of picking cotton.

As the sharecroppers discussed how joining the union would help one another and finally secure financial power, carloads of white men, "of which there were several," drove toward the church. Two white law officers loaded their guns and hopped into a Model T Ford. They reached the church before midnight and cut the engine. As the guards walked toward them, the officers opened fire.

While shots rang out "like popcorn popping" and bullets flew past their heads, the sharecroppers inside the church rushed to find safety—crashing through windows and seeking

Arkansas Governor Charles Brough (center right) addresses a white crowd in Elaine.

cover in the delta thicket. Ed Ware fell to the floor and Frank Moore crumpled on top of him as "bullets just kept raining through the house."

It all happened so quickly, and when the shooting was over, white law officer W. A. Adkins was dead.

The next day, the mayor of Elaine frantically telegrammed the governor of Arkansas with an urgent plea for help. The town was under

Governor Brough, right, meets with Camp Pike commander Colonel Isaac Jenks.

siege, the mayor claimed, by rioting Black Americans. Nothing could have been further from the truth.

For several terrifying hours, Ed Ware hid in the rivercane lining the frigid, swampy marshes before making his way to his cabin. He had no way of knowing who had died in the church, but when he reached his house and saw a posse of white men with guns racing through his fields, he knew he had to leave—fast. Had he stayed near the shooting scene in Hoop Spur, he would have witnessed how quickly flames engulfed the wooden building. Eager to torch the church, a posse of white men had set fire to it, removing any evidence of broken glass and that the walls had been peppered with bullets.

While the mayor waited to hear from the governor, hundreds of white men from other states crossed the Mississippi River with loaded guns—and some with axes. They'd been summoned by local officials to crush what Arkansas newspapers called a "Negro plot to rise against the white residents." They joined

Black men and women who survived the bloodshed were rounded up and marched to jail.

local posses and tore through the area, searching for Black men, women, and children—and shooting them.

No tally was kept of the dead. Was it twenty-three people or a thousand? Newspapers wrote that nineteen African Americans were killed, yet burials would climb to more than two hundred. Years later, a local journalist claimed the death toll was closer to nine hundred. We'll never know the exact number, except for the number of white deaths—and that tally would become five. What is certain is that what happened in and around Elaine, Arkansas, in the first few days of October 1919, was not a race riot, as the press kept calling it. It was a massacre conducted by angry mobs of white Americans.

Ed Ware swiftly made his way to Louisiana as Arkansas Governor Charles Brough responded to the crisis. On Thursday, October 2, Brough called in federal troops from nearby Camp Pike—where Frank Moore had been stationed the year before—and rode on a train with five hundred white soldiers to Elaine. Treating this like a war, they brought with them twelve machine guns, gas masks, and hand grenades. Any Black man was rounded up, arrested, and marched past cornfields that rose so high they hid the numbers of those arrested and the brutality of the day.

"They were shooting at us all the time . . . I took the children and the women and went to the woods and stayed until the next morning," Moore recalled. As an army veteran, Moore felt relief when he spotted soldiers from Camp Pike. He led the women and children out of the woods and told the soldiers he was a veteran, but they apprehended Moore and

We Print
THE TRUTH
No Matter Whom
IT HURTS

Chicago
WORLD'S

VOL. XIV   NO. 45 ★★   SATURDAY   CHIC

SIX DEATH VERDI

Arkansas Court Acts Like
Whirlwind in Dispens=
ing "Justice"

False coverage in the *Arkansas Gazette* stirred up anti-Black sentiment. In contrast, the *Chicago Defender* mocked the court's system of "justice."

VICIOUS BLACKS WERE PLANNING GREAT UPRISING

All Evidence Points to Carefully Prepared Rebellion

BEGUN PREMATURELY

Blacks Suspected Officers Who Stopped Near Church by Accident.

Defender

WEEKLY

OUR PRINCIPLES
Racial Uplift and
Obedience to Law.

BER 8. 1919   SATURDAY   PRICE FIVE CENTS

IN EIGHT MINUTES

imprisoned him. Other federal troops gunned down Black people, including World War veterans.

The president of the Hoop Spur union had already been murdered and many union members shot. Approximately 225 Black men and women were held in a school in Elaine while a mob of white people surrounded the building, their eyes filled with hate.

The scene proved no different at the county jail in Helena, where the men considered the most dangerous and responsible for the deaths of the white men were locked up. There, Governor Brough promised justice to quiet the vengeful crowd by appointing a Committee of Seven to decide the fates of the prisoners. As the mayor, the sheriff, and the landowners who formed the committee shook hands with the governor, newspapers proclaimed that the "Elaine Insurrection" was over.

The Committee of Seven swiftly issued a bulletin "To the Negroes of Phillips County," claiming that no innocent Black people had been arrested and that everyone else had nothing to fear, even though no white people had been arrested for the killings. The bulletin told them to go back to work "as if nothing had happened," demanding that they:

STOP TALKING!
Stay at home—Go to work—Don't worry!

A month later, eighty-six sharecroppers were hastily tried in the county courthouse in Helena. Some of the jurors had taken part in killing and terrorizing the victims, including white veterans from the American Legion.

Within minutes, Frank Moore and ten other prisoners were convicted of murder. Ed Ware would soon become number twelve. He'd made it safely into Louisiana and briefly stayed alive by foraging for persimmons, then took a job as a wagon driver, making deliveries. But he'd been arrested in New Orleans and hauled into Helena for an eight-minute trial. Now he was on death row, too, same as the

TO THE NEGROES
OF PHILLIPS COUNTY
Helena, Ark., Oct. 7, 1919

The trouble at Hoop Spur and Elaine has been settled.

Soldiers now here to preserve order will return to Little Rock within a short time.

No innocent negro has been arrested, and those of you who are at home and at work have no occasion to worry.

All you have to do is to remain at work just as if nothing had happened.

Phillips County has always been a peaceful, lawabiding community, and normal conditions must be restored right away.

STOP TALKING!
Stay at home---Go to work---Don't worry!

F. F. KITCHENS, Sheriff   COMMITTEE
Edward Bevens J. C. Meyers S. Straub E. M. Allen
T. W. Keesee D. A. Keeshan Amos Jarman
H. D. Moore J. G. Knight Jno. L. Moore E. C. Hornor

Nicholls Print, Helena, Ark.

The Committee of Seven issued this notice shortly after the massacre.

other eleven men, sentenced to die in a month by electric chair. Seventy-five others were sent to the state penitentiary or the Cummins State Prison Farm, sentenced to years of hard labor.

It seemed impossible that the twelve men would escape death, let alone be freed. Except, that is, in the mind of a man raised 140 miles from the carnage. Though Scipio Jones was a churchgoer like the convicted sharecroppers, he didn't pray for a miracle. He believed in the power of laws.

As thick, iron chains were shackled onto the wrists and ankles of the Elaine Twelve men and they boarded a freight train to the state penitentiary, Scipio was on his way to Helena to save them.

SCIPIO JONES.

December 1919
Little Rock

The man most interested in the cases headed toward the hissing train with trepidation. He wore a Panama hat and a suit with a dangling gold pocket watch, and his full name was Scipio Africanus Jones. Friends warned him not to go to Helena, that it was much too dangerous for the attorney. But if he did go, he should do so in the stillness of the night to protect himself from the prying eyes of white people.

Black professionals, not just sharecroppers, were now being accused of causing a race riot. A dentist and his war-hero brothers had been murdered in Elaine after stepping off a train. The lynchings happened in broad daylight. In the midst of this powder keg of racial tension, a white professional, Ocier

Bratton—from the law firm that Ed Ware had hired—arrived in October ready to meet with sharecroppers, but was arrested and thrown in jail. Reviled as a traitor to his own race, Bratton had been warned that he'd be lynched, too.

Nothing was going to stop Scipio Jones from representing the Elaine Twelve or gathering the information he needed to defend them. Leaning on a cane—perhaps to relieve the twitch in his neck that caused a slight tremor—Scipio proceeded through the billowing clouds of engine steam and boarded the train for Helena. A Black man traveling to the most racially charged town in America wouldn't be welcome, especially a lawyer who sought to defend the innocence of the Elaine Twelve. The twelve were hailed by many in Black communities across the country as heroes and viewed as villains in most white ones.

But the biggest mistake a person of any color could make was underestimating Scipio Jones.

In his late fifties by 1919, Scipio had thinning hair and a moustache the color of salt and pepper. We don't know exactly when he was born since he rarely spoke about his childhood. Historians think his mother, Jemmima, gave birth to him in a covered wagon in 1863. Enslaved by a plantation owner, she'd been forced to have a child with him, and Scipio was born. Nicknamed Sippi, he'd been born into slavery, too. When emancipation drew near and Jemmima could legally marry her partner, Horace, they chose the last name of Jones.

After the Civil War, the family moved to Tulip, Arkansas. While the war officially ended slavery, the system essentially survived in the South through local segregation laws and discriminatory practices known as Jim Crow. As a kid, Scipio and his brothers and sisters picked cotton, and he made the most of the time between harvests by attending school.

Well aware of segregation and suppression, Scipio refused to let those practices strip him of his dignity or stop his dream of becoming a lawyer. He fought back with his intelligence and moved to Little Rock, where he graduated from Bethel Institute (now Shorter College). When the whites-only University of Arkansas refused to let him study law, he took control by boldly approaching a group of white attorneys and asking if he could be their apprentice. They agreed, and Scipio learned the law by studying their books at night while teaching school by day.

Scipio became adept at functioning on a few hours' sleep, sometimes snoozing on pool tables when he couldn't find lodging. After passing the bar exam, he declined to take the safe route of writing up wills. Instead, he became a trial attorney in a state where most courtrooms allowed Black lawyers to argue cases only if white lawyers appeared to be in charge.

Scipio's ability to convincingly articulate the law and clearly describe the unfolding of events helped people see the truth—and sometimes side with it. As the first Black lawyer to argue appeals in the Arkansas Supreme Court, he fought railroad segregation, stopped laws preventing Black people from voting, and became the first lawyer in the state to use the Fourteenth Amendment to the Constitution in arguing against convictions. That amendment gave equal protections to all citizens, regardless of their race.

Scipio's confident, positive attitude and strong sense of

justice mesmerized clients and even opponents. "His word was 'gilt edged,'" said one Little Rock attorney, who called Scipio "a man of the highest principles."

When asked to fill in for a municipal judge in court one day, Scipio became known as Judge Jones. His practice thrived and his clients included prominent Black fraternal organizations such as the Mosaic Templars of America and the Order of the Eastern Star. The thirty-five oak bookcases in his office bulged with case files, and Scipio became quite wealthy. He purchased at least eight rental properties, and since he never did learn to drive, he hired a chauffeur to shuttle him around Little Rock in a Cadillac.

Scipio soared to superhero status in Black communities, where kids pretended to be Judge Jones. Inspired by his success, a young girl impersonated Scipio in front of her brothers. "Justice!" she demanded, throwing her arms up in the air. "All I ask of you, gentlemen of the jury, is justice."

Scipio was willing to fight for justice to the death. And he knew that the only way the Elaine Twelve wouldn't die was if he went to Helena and did everything he could to prove their innocence. In fact, as jailers handed the convicted men their death row uniforms, Scipio was already hard at work discussing ways of freeing them with a group of Black attorneys in Little Rock. As one of the best defense lawyers and courtroom cross-examiners in the South, there was no question that Scipio would be the prisoners' attorney. Everyone chipped in money for a defense fund to cover legal costs and agreed that Scipio would take control of the cases.

That's why it came as a shock when a letter appeared in a

city newspaper congratulating Governor Brough for stopping an insurrection and restoring law and order. The surprise was that it was signed by Scipio Jones. Had Scipio turned his back on justice—on civil and constitutional rights? Absolutely not. He was certain that there hadn't been an uprising—at least not on the part of Black Arkansans, and that the men hadn't killed anyone. But he needed to gather evidence to prove it, and he couldn't do that if the men were dead.

Scipio had to recruit as many allies as he could—especially powerful, white allies like Brough—to keep the men alive. He knew the governor could stop, or at the very least, delay the electrocutions until Scipio could implement his grandest and most ambitious plan—taking the cases to the highest court in the country—the U.S. Supreme Court. But first he'd have to push for new trials in Arkansas courts.

He had to act quickly. When Scipio boarded the train for Helena, the executions were only a few weeks away. Helena's sheriff certainly couldn't be considered an ally; he was part of the Committee of Seven who'd rigged the hasty trials. But Scipio wasn't intimidated. In his diplomatic and transparent manner, he contacted the sheriff and told him of his plans to visit the mercurial town.

The main reason Scipio rushed to Helena was to meet the relatives of the Elaine Twelve. First, he planned to assure them that he was doing everything in his power to free their loved ones. Second, he planned to give them the option of moving to Little Rock so they could visit their husbands, sons, and daddies in jail every Sunday. Scipio had set aside his own money for this. Most importantly, since many of the family members had attended the union meeting the night of the shooting, he hoped to convince them to testify in court, if he could secure new trials. Scipio strongly believed their accounts would save their relatives' lives.

It didn't take long for Ed Ware's wife, Lula, to decide to move to Little Rock. Her life was entwined with Ed's, and it had been just the two of them these past few years. Lula had also been jailed for attending the Hoop Spur union meeting. When she'd finally been released, Lula walked the twenty miles to their cabin. She found their treasured heirloom mirror riddled with bullets, the safe stolen, their farm animals—her Jersey cow, the 135 chickens—and Ed's prized automobile used for taxi driving, gone.

Scipio had seen the decimated cabins and learned that most of the women had been forced off the land that they'd cultivated with their husbands. But Lula's story had additional heartache. She and Ed had moved to Arkansas from Louisiana to start life over after all their children died of illnesses like "the fever." Scipio understood that kind of despair. His first wife, Carrie, had died young, but thankfully they'd had a precious child together—his only child, a daughter named Hazel—to remind him of her. And he'd done his best to raise Hazel on his own.

Lula Ware didn't have anyone but Ed. And with her new life in Arkansas now destroyed, she longed to be as close to her husband as she could and agreed to testify at a new trial.

Lula and the other sharecroppers' wives gave Scipio vivid testimony on how they'd been ambushed and shot at during the

Wives and mothers worked as hard as the men and joined the union to demand economic justice.

union meeting and how people had been killed in the church. A young mother showed Scipio her swollen arm where a bullet still remained lodged in the flesh. After shots were fired and broken glass rained down on the sharecroppers and their wives, she'd knelt on the floor, protecting her baby in her arms, grateful that the bullet hadn't hit the child. The women told of seeing white posse members gunning down Black sharecroppers in the days following the ambush. Frank Moore's wife fled when her landlord threatened to kill her if she didn't leave.

It was clear to Scipio that this was no insurrection on the part of Black Arkansans, but a killing spree to stop them from demanding fair prices for their harvests. Because these women had also stood up for their rights, the crops they'd cultivated with their husbands had been snatched away by landowners who refused to pay for them. Their possessions had been destroyed and their loved ones locked in jail, sentenced to die.

After the interviews, Scipio boarded the Yazoo and Mississippi Valley Railroad train back to Little Rock, riding through woodlands so thick and so close to the train "that one scarcely sees the sun." Suddenly, open fields came into view, those very fields where sharecroppers had been killed while "picking cotton, harming nobody." Scipio wrote that "a large number of negroes were killed, from 50 to 60." But the death toll turned out to be much higher.

Early newspaper reports of the massacre told that two of the five white men killed had died after accidentally being fired on by their own posse, or when their own guns had gone off by mistake. But those truths were now being ignored. The telegraph lines from Helena had been suspiciously cut, and the only communication from the city came from the Committee of Seven, who claimed those early reports were fake. Scipio knew that the committee needed a reason to convict the union sharecroppers, and that they'd crafted lies to make it look as if a Black uprising had occurred. They falsely claimed that proof of a conspiracy had been discovered in the church before it was burned down: an actual list of white landowners the union members planned

A family of sharecroppers gathers on their porch near Little Rock. Many found their homes ransacked after the massacre.

ELAINE RIOTERS, WHO WERE BROUGHT TO PEN TO PAY DEATH PENALTY IN CHAIR

Left to right: Ed Hicks, Ed Coleman, Ed Ware, Frank Moore, Paul Hall, Albert Giles, Joe Knox, Frank Hicks, Joe Fox, Alfred Banks Jr., John Martin and William Wordlow.

Arkansas newspapers closely followed the trials but never reported how unfair they were.

to kill in order to steal their property. What troubled Scipio was that "the minds of the white people were deeply imbued with the belief that all this stuff was true."

The local newspaper even published a bizarre and hastily written statement called *Inward Facts About Negro Insurrection*. The statement was riddled with racist language. In it, the Committee of Seven wrote that not only were some of their own names on the list, but they'd seen it for themselves. The statement said that every Black person who joined the union "was given to kill white people." But where, Scipio wanted to know, was this alleged list? He'd already pored over the trial records and knew that it had never been produced or admitted as evidence.

What Scipio had was new and *real* evidence: first-person accounts from women sharecroppers about the night of the shooting, and their bullet scars to prove it. Now he needed to focus on getting more of the truth directly from the Elaine Twelve men.

THE ELAINE TWELVE

The Elaine Twelve men

Alf Banks farmed 32 acres of cotton. He had just reached his twentieth birthday.

Ed Coleman was born into slavery in 1841 and was by far the oldest of the men at age 78. He had 18 acres of cotton and was married, with many grandchildren.

Joe Fox was 22 years old and had 20 acres of cotton.

Albert Giles attended the union meeting with his teenage brother and their mother, Sallie.

Paul Hall farmed 40 acres of cotton.

Ed Hicks and his wife, Arrieta, had three daughters. He was a leader of the effort to unionize.

Frank Hicks served as a union leader, like his brother, Ed.

All of these men were sharecroppers, cultivating cotton and other crops in the fields near Elaine, Arkansas. Most of them were Baptists or Methodists, and several had served in the U.S. military. None had ever been convicted of a crime. NAACP official Ida B. Wells-Barnett estimated that the twelve men had harvested at least $100,000 worth of cotton and other crops in the autumn of 1919. They lost all of it.

Joe Knox and his wife, Katie, had a son and two daughters. Friends called Joe "Preacher."

John Martin farmed 22 acres of cotton. He was married, with five children.

Frank Moore was a husband and father who'd been honorably discharged from the U.S. Army in 1918.

Ed Ware served as the union secretary, grew cotton, and ran a private taxi business. His cotton crop was worth more than $20,000 in 1919.

Will Wordlow was 22 years old and worked 16 acres. He and his wife, Willie Bell, had just become parents. (In some documents, their last name is spelled Wardlow or Wordlaw).

The Elaine Twelve were imprisoned in two death-house jail cells at The Walls—the state penitentiary outside Little Rock. An arm's length away, on the other side of their cell walls, sat the oak-and-leather electric chair cruelly nicknamed "Old Sparky."

The men were scheduled to be strapped into that chair and killed by electric currents. They were eager to tell their stories to an attorney who was interested in knowing the truth and would fight to save them.

Each man wore the standard prison uniform, with brown denim overalls and a matching cap. Scipio shook hands with them through the bars of the freshly painted cells, then pulled up a chair and began asking questions. The men had to speak quietly; a security guard stood fifty feet away.

Listening intently, Scipio learned the grim facts. As the white mob stormed the Helena jail that night in October, they'd intended to kill the Black sharecroppers who'd been arrested. The Committee of Seven let the mob in, then locked the doors of the red-brick building. With Camp Pike troops standing guard over the cells to protect the sharecroppers from being lynched, the committee made it clear that there was no need to murder the men right then and there. They gave the mob this "solemn promise": The sharecroppers would be found guilty of murder and killed by electrocution until, as the judge at the trials proclaimed, they were "dead, dead, dead."

As the men confirmed to Scipio that the speedy convictions had been predetermined, it now made sense to him why the sheriff had let Scipio come to Helena without incident: because the committee had orchestrated everything. They were in control, and they believed that no one—including a skillful lawyer like Scipio Jones—was going to stop them.

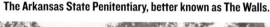

The Arkansas State Penitentiary, better known as The Walls.

The prisoners described how they'd been terrorized after the pact was made. When their interrogators questioned them about the night of the union meeting, all the men stated that they had nothing to do with the killings and had never been jailed before. During the ambush they'd grabbed their guns and fled for safety.

"I went in the woods and stayed all night," recalled Will Wordlow, who said he did not have a gun. "I had eight women and children with me to hide, keep them from getting killed. The white people sent word all through the county that they were coming to kill all the Negroes they could find."

Three of the men revealed to Scipio that they'd been shot by posse members as they lay motionless in the canebrakes, seeking shelter from the massacre. Albert Giles had been shot not once, but five times. He showed Scipio the spot in his skull where a bullet had entered, and he pointed to the place near his left ear where it exited.

This kind of testimony hadn't been what the Committee of Seven wanted to hear, so the men were taken to the top floor of the jailhouse and "whipped nearly to death" with leather straps.

Alf Banks described being whipped three times and shocked in an electric chair. "I have the scars on my body to show now."

Though the wounds were healing, the men rolled up their shirts and showed Scipio the jagged scars on their backs and hips. "So terror-inspiring were the whippings," Scipio wrote after he'd looked away from their mangled flesh, "that not a word of it leaked out in the proceedings."

Scipio learned from the prisoners that posse members
had acted lawlessly during the rampage in Elaine.

He could have added that the threats on their lives were still so palpable that the men hadn't told anyone about the torture, except now—to Scipio. What's more, they could identify their torturers, including a law officer by the name of Henry Smiddy. Since the sharecroppers hadn't killed anyone and there obviously wasn't any evidence that they had, the only way the Committee of Seven could have them convicted was, as the men told Scipio, "to make us lie" about each other. So Smiddy and others whipped, drugged, and zapped them with electric shocks—there was some sort of gruesome replica of Old Sparky at the county jail—until they made false confessions.

To further seal their fate at the November trials, the men had been assigned court-appointed attorneys who made no attempts to speak with them, gather evidence, or change the trial location. As Scipio asked about the proceedings, it became obvious that the sharecroppers had been given no "definite idea of their rights." During their lightning-fast trials, they'd been found guilty by a jury of all white men. They had, as Scipio carefully noted, been deprived of every right "under the Constitution, and especially the Fourteenth Amendment."

There had been no equal protection under the law for the Elaine Twelve, and Scipio intended for every one of them to testify about their chilling ordeals at new trials. He just had to make sure that they would get them. Scipio needed to make it clear that none of the men's previous confessions were true, nor were any claims they'd made about other defendants. As Frank Moore said, he and others had been "put in an electric chair and shocked to make us lie [about] each other."

Scipio filed a motion for new trials on December 20—seven days before the first scheduled electrocutions. They were flatly denied by the same judge who had ruled over every sham trial in November.

Now it was time for Scipio's letter that publicly praised Governor Brough to take effect. Brough assured Arkansans that while the trials had been fair, it wouldn't hurt to have the Arkansas Supreme Court confirm this. So he agreed to delay the executions, paving the way for Scipio to appeal the verdicts.

The Elaine Twelve had escaped death, but only temporarily. Scipio had found them more time. Now he needed to get more money to prepare the appeals, to keep the Elaine Twelve families in Little Rock, and to hire another attorney to work around the clock with him on the cases.

Scipio hoped to secure financial help from the NAACP: the National Association for the Advancement of Colored People. What he didn't expect was that the biggest civil rights group in America had different plans.

Journalist and anti-lynching crusader Ida B. Wells-Barnett secretly interviewed the men in prison.

Though it had been founded only ten years before, in 1909, the NAACP was the largest and most effective civil rights group in the country, pushing for the obliteration of class and race discrimination. Scipio would later give speeches on the organization's behalf, but at this point he certainly wasn't known at its national headquarters in New York City.

Sociologist W. E. B. Du Bois, the most influential Black civil rights leader of the day, helped start the NAACP and ran its magazine, *The Crisis*. Equally famous women's rights activist and anti-lynching crusader Ida B. Wells-Barnett sat on the board as a founding member. But most of the NAACP's founders were white, including the president, Moorfield Storey, an

Walter White of the NAACP posed as a white reporter to uncover facts about the massacre.

attorney from Boston who handled the biggest cases involving constitutional law.

The association had never fought against state court verdicts—until the Elaine Twelve. Usually, the NAACP shined a spotlight on racial injustices by bringing media attention to them. That awareness created outrage and sometimes change. NAACP employees, like Walter White, even went undercover to get at the truth.

White became an expert on lynching cases. Because he was a light-skinned Black man, he traveled the country passing as a white person and covering the horrors as a reporter for *The Chicago Daily News*. But going to Helena, Arkansas, terrified him, even though he knew he'd have to go because of the Elaine Twelve. These cases had the potential of rocking the country's constitutional foundation. The NAACP *had* to get involved.

White later wrote that visiting Helena was the scariest experience of his life. Too frightened to interview the sheriff or the Committee of Seven because he thought he'd be lynched himself, White ended up reporting on the real reason for the massacre anyway: to keep Black farmers under the control of the powerful landowners (or *in peonage*) and deny their right to negotiate the best prices for their crops.

White also had his own prejudice—against Scipio Jones. It turns out that Walter White was a bit of a snob. White, born in the city of Atlanta, worried about having a country lawyer like Scipio in charge. Without even knowing of Scipio's accomplishments in the courtroom, White pictured him as a bungling, small-town attorney who wouldn't be capable of handling the cases or taking them all the way to the U.S. Supreme Court. What he wanted was for a white attorney to be in control, and he said as much.

But that wasn't going to happen.

To be fair, Walter White wanted to win. And going by courtroom records in the early 1900s in a divided America, winning criminal cases involving Black defendants typically meant having a white attorney in charge—especially in the segregated South. But Scipio wasn't typical, and neither were the Elaine Twelve cases.

Scipio knew the history of Arkansas trials as well as anyone. And he'd hired Colonel George W. Murphy—a seventy-nine-year-old white lawyer and former Confederate Civil War officer—to assist him. When Scipio was born into slavery, Colonel Murphy was fighting to preserve enslavement as the way of life in the South! But somewhere along the way he'd had a change of heart, and over the years he'd shown his commitment to social justice. He and Scipio battled each other in court a few times, and they had great mutual respect. Scipio welcomed Murphy's assistance.

Perhaps the strangest part of this story so far is that the NAACP had *also* hired Murphy, and both Murphy and the NAACP kept that a secret from Scipio. The NAACP kept its involvement hush-hush, because there could be repercussions if, as they put it, "a northern organization was known to be financing" the appeals.

But the NAACP's secret couldn't be kept for long, and their true wish—to have Murphy take control of the case—would never materialize. With Scipio being the "heart and center of the defense," Murphy wrote to the NAACP to make clear that Scipio was in charge, and that was that. From then on Scipio and the NAACP would pool their money and their resources for one purpose—to free the Elaine Twelve men.

The story of the men drew national attention. Black-owned newspapers and magazines voiced their outrage against the massacre—but they didn't call it that at first. It was still being labeled "a race riot" or described as "an uprising." But after Walter White visited Helena and wrote about how peonage had caused the lynching of Black Americans and that Helena was hell for people of color, the Black press began writing how equality had been crushed and that the verdicts of the Elaine Twelve men were decided by white jurors who were enemies of humanity. These kinds of headlines had exactly the explosive impact that the NAACP worried about. The articles irritated Arkansas Governor Brough so much that he began blaming the NAACP and northern newspapers for inciting the massacre. He called for their publications to be banned in his state. But that didn't happen either.

Ida B. Wells-Barnett wrote about the Elaine Twelve in *The Chicago Defender* and held a protest to raise money for their defense. When Lula Ware brought the articles to The Walls for her husband to read, he immediately wrote a note of thanks. Soon, Wells-Barnett arrived at The Walls for a

Ida B. Wells-Barnett published her findings after interviewing the Elaine Twelve men.

personal visit, but she had to pretend to be a relative visiting one of the men. Prison officials would never have let her in if they'd known who she was.

Scipio and the men gave Wells-Barnett detailed information about the cases. The men were lonely and afraid, and Ed Ware lamented that he had "no friends at all." Despite what the Black-owned newspapers wrote, many people had turned away from them, fearing that any show of support would endanger their own lives.

The men prayed and sang every day in their death-house cells. Scipio was deeply affected by their spiritual devotion. The singing, Scipio wrote, "would move any audience to tears."

Ed Ware composed a hymn describing their plight called "I Stand and Wring My Hands and Cry." It cut to the bone. "With my enemies all crushing me and confusion in my home: I then fold my arms and look to the skies," Ed sang, "And I just stand and wring my hands and cry." The melody and words of the somber song carried to the warden's home next to the prison and he, too, came quietly to the death house and listened to the heartbreaking chorus.

Determined to save the men, Scipio scrutinized the trial transcripts and court records, searching for a breakthrough. He knew about the moral injustices, but because of the grip of white supremacy, he needed to find a legal mistake that could cause the verdicts to be overturned. And there it was—right in front of him—the monumental, game-changing discovery he needed. The Helena jurors had been in such a hurry to convict the Elaine Twelve for murder that in six of the cases they neglected to say what *kind* of murder. In Arkansas, you couldn't charge a person with murder unless you stipulated the *degree* of murder—first or second.

Scipio knew immediately that six of the men would most certainly be granted new trials. But as ecstatic as he was about this development, Scipio knew that the history of defending Black people in court by holding up the Fourteenth Amendment—which included the right to a fair trial—had been dismal.

Things didn't look good for the other six men, as they'd been convicted of murder in the first degree. But Scipio never lost faith that constitutional law would finally be put into practice for Black people.

On March 29, 1920, when the Arkansas Supreme Court handed down its ruling on the appeals of the twelve condemned men, both hope and sadness filled Scipio's heart. There would be new trials in May for six of the men because of the legal mistake Scipio had uncovered. But the fate of the other six men stood firm. The court wrote that those trials had been fair. And since these men had fled their homes with their guns the day after the deadly union meeting—in self-defense or not—the justices reasoned that this proved they were guilty of a conspiracy and "the possible killing of white men."

The Elaine Twelve were now on two very different tracks. As it stood, six men had a chance of living and six were more likely to die.

Ed Ware and the other men who'd been convicted of murder without degree would come to be known as the *Ware*

Six. They included Alf Banks, John Martin, Will Wordlow, Albert Giles, and Joe Fox.

Veteran soldier Frank Moore and his five colleagues—Preacher Joe Knox, Paul Hall, brothers Ed Hicks and Frank Hicks, and Ed Coleman, who was more than a half century older than many of the men—came to be referred to as the *Moore Six*. Each had been convicted of first-degree murder.

The two distinct groups meant separate cases and different jails. The Moore men remained in the death house at The Walls, where at least they were let outside each day for fresh air and exercise. The Ware men returned to the torturous hell in Helena, sleeping on cold concrete floors in the Phillips County jail until their retrials a little more than a month later.

But there was one unifying factor that would prove to be the most essential: All of them still had the same lawyer and the best chance of survival in Scipio Jones.

Ever the optimist, even in the face of death, Scipio focused on the most valuable truth that linked the men—their innocence. If Scipio could get one group of six acquitted, then surely the others would have to be freed, too. But—and here was the scary part—this logic also worked the other way. If the Moore men were executed, then surely the Ware men would be, too.

Scipio walked a legal tightrope, with time ticking on one end and the biased history of constitutional law on the other. What's more, there were only twenty-four hours in a day—and Scipio's workload had just been doubled, courtesy of the Arkansas Supreme Court.

May 1920
Helena, Arkansas

On the first weekend of May, Scipio and Colonel Murphy traveled by train from Little Rock to Helena. They couldn't ride in the same rail car together, as nearly every facet of life in the South was segregated. And they would have to lodge in different places, too, meeting in front of the Phillips County Courthouse first thing Monday morning, May 3, for day one of the retrials of Ed Ware and the five men who'd been sentenced with him back in November.

For their new trials, the Ware men would be facing Judge J. M. Jackson—the same judge who had condemned them to death six months earlier—and the same relentless prosecutor, John Miller. He'd pushed hard for their death sentences, conjuring up witnesses willing to lie. Perhaps more than anything, Jackson, Miller, and the other men in charge of Helena's courtrooms detested being shown up and proven wrong. The truth didn't matter. Revenge did.

The white men of Helena crammed into the courtroom seats. They simmered with anger and humiliation over the verdicts being questioned by the Arkansas Supreme Court on a technicality. They'd expected the condemned sharecroppers to be dead by now. Instead, they were very much alive.

John Martin stood a few feet from the crowd, anxious to testify at his new trial. All of the men would be testifying about the torture and how they'd been terrorized into lying in the earlier trials.

"We must win," Scipio knew. "These men have lived under the shadow of the electric chair long enough."

Since Helena was separated by race, the courtroom was, too. Upstairs in a gallery, high above the white residents, Black Arkansans focused on catching a glimpse of Scipio Jones. For this time, unlike the first trials, the Ware men had Scipio defending them. And all of the men would be taking the witness stand to tell the truth. No more false statements made under torture refuting their innocence. Instead, they would tell about the torture and how they'd been terrorized *because* of their innocence.

Scipio had prepared a convincing defense, detailing how unfair the previous trials had been—from the manufactured testimony of white witnesses who told of an insurrection but couldn't produce any evidence, to the forced, self-incriminating statements of his clients. It all stemmed, Scipio wrote, from "an intense prejudice against them on account of their color."

Scipio had new affidavits from the Ware men stating their innocence and the reason why their earlier statements were false—because they'd been made out of fear following days of gruesome torture. Obviously, this news would signal a huge red flag that would certainly bring gasps from the audience. Could the jury possibly deny the Ware men their freedom after listening to the ways they'd been brutalized into making those statements? Scipio hoped that they wouldn't. And though always ready to argue on the floor in his suit and bowtie, all he could do was settle into his wooden chair at the defense table and listen. Colonel Murphy would be delivering the defense that Scipio had so painstakingly prepared. Even though Scipio was in charge, the unwritten rules of segregation demanded that the lead attorney be white.

Colonel George Murphy served in the Confederate Army during the Civil War, but he proved to be an able assistant to Scipio in defense of the Elaine Twelve.

Just as he began to state the defense's case, Colonel Murphy opened his mouth and froze. He clutched his hand to his chest—and crumpled to the ground!

Splayed out on the courtroom floor, Murphy looked dead. As guards hoisted him out of the courtroom, nervous whispers that he'd been poisoned raced through the room. Were Helena whites so incensed that the previous verdicts had been overturned that they'd poisoned the assistant defense attorney? And if Murphy had been killed, would Scipio be next?

Scipio had to take over the defense *by himself*—without a white "front man." Of course, Scipio had really been in charge all along: He'd written the arguments, done all the research, and developed relationships with the sharecroppers. But he wasn't in Little Rock anymore, where he'd gained respect, chipping through decades of racism. He was in hostile territory. And as much as the lives of the Ware men were in question, Scipio's life was in danger, too.

It turned out that Colonel Murphy was alive. He hadn't been poisoned after all. He'd suffered a heart attack, but his days as a courtroom attorney were over. Scipio's were just beginning in Phillips County.

Scipio calmly took hold of the proceedings. Before every case, he requested a change of venue, asking that the "talesmen"— jurors pulled in off the street—be dismissed, the cases be transferred to federal court, and the entire jury be set aside because there wasn't a single Black person in the jury pool. With Black residents outnumbering the white population of Helena five to one, "A great many of them . . ." Scipio reminded the judge, had "qualifications being equal to those of the whites."

Each time Scipio filed these motions, Judge Jackson promptly denied them, and the new trials began.

Prosecutor Miller called his primary white witness—

Charles Pratt, who'd been in the Model T Ford driving up to the Hoop Spur church with W.A. Adkins during the union meeting. Pratt said that when they'd pulled in near the church, a group of Black men asked him if his car wasn't working, a statement that Scipio quickly seized upon during his cross examination. Scipio explained that the question was "a civil one, [and] indicated a desire to help." Pratt's accusation of aggression by the Black armed guards had been deflated by a single Scipio conclusion. By the time Scipio finished his cross-examination, he'd managed to get Pratt to admit that "everybody shot," and that the church had purposely been burned down.

Miller called Henry Smiddy, the torturer, to the witness stand. Smiddy insisted there were "no bullet holes at all in the church," even though Pratt had just admitted that there'd been shooting on the part of whites. Now the prosecution's argument contradicted itself. And when Miller called Black witnesses to the stand expecting them to incriminate the Ware men as they'd done in the first trials, they shocked the courtroom by admitting that they'd lied earlier about the sharecroppers' guilt because they'd been tortured, too.

Scipio kept puncturing holes in the prosecution's arguments and exposing how the testimonies were contradictory, vague, and flimsy. And when Will Wordlow took the stand in his own defense, he verbally sparred with Miller, daring him to discuss the torture. "If you don't believe I have any scars on me," he told the prosecutor, "I will let my clothes down and let you see it."

Scipio continued to ask the most logical questions—such

In many families, both the husband and wife joined the sharecroppers' union.

as, for instance, since the Ware men could name their torturers, why hadn't the prosecution questioned these lawmen on the witness stand about what had happened "if it was not in every respect true?"

"The trouble about it," Scipio knew, "was that it was all true." Earlier in the trial, Scipio had forced Judge Jackson to acknowledge the torture, but the judge only allowed discussion about it without the jury or the newspapers present.

As the day's proceedings drew to a close, the prosecution seemed sunk and Scipio and the defense victorious. But with the sun setting, Scipio was faced with a new problem—his own safety. He'd made the prosecution look ridiculous, and the animosity and rage were clear throughout the courtroom.

There was no chauffeur waiting outside to whisk him away. Years before, Scipio had slept on pool tables when he had no other place to go. But here in this angry town, he needed something much more secure.

A home was best—nine different homes for the nine nights of the trials so no one could track him down.

Scipio left the courthouse and—as he would do each night in Helena—slipped into a drugstore owned by Black merchants and asked for a safe place to sleep. Perhaps it would be a Black family's home nearby, or miles away in the country. Names were never recorded, because Scipio knew that with every cross-examination, every hour that ticked away in the Phillips County courtroom defending his clients, his time in Helena grew more dangerous, and so did the lives of the families who let him stay in their homes.

In the morning, whether he'd slept five minutes away or fifteen, Scipio arrived at the courthouse unrattled and ready for another battle of words. And he would defend the truth using the front doors—not back doors. He walked up the steps to the main entrance of the courthouse and continued to slice through the weak cases against his clients. He exposed every rendition of corruption, deceit, and barbarism for the world to see.

Disgusted by the strength of the defense proceedings, Arkansas newspapers like the *Helena World* covered the retrials less and less. They didn't write that during the week of the trials, Lula Ware told how she and the union members had been shot at while in the church. Or how she described the days that followed when white posse members were looking to kill them. That's why they'd all had to flee for their lives.

The newspapers didn't mention how Scipio saved the most compelling witness for last: the mother who'd clung so tightly to the baby in her arms as she dropped to her knees, crawling on the church floor that was shattered with glass from gunfire. She told how a bullet had struck her, and that it was still lodged in her arm. And there was nothing written in the papers about Joe Fox or Albert Giles taking the stand, telling in detail about rushing to temporary safety in the canebrakes, and how they'd heard misfiring posse members surrounding them in a circle yelling that they were "killing our own men."

Finally, Scipio held up union documents like the ones discovered at the Hoop Spur church and explained how they told of organizing for equal rights, not of murdering white landowners. Then he asked the most obvious question every spectator in the courtroom must have been thinking—where was the list of white landowners to be killed that the sharecroppers supposedly had written and the Committee of Seven claimed to have as evidence?

"Is it not striking," Scipio declared, "that not a single incriminating paper, was offered or introduced into evidence?"

A fter everything Scipio had done to prove the innocence of the Ware men, the jurors came to the same verdict for all six: "We, the jury, find the defendant guilty of murder in the first degree," they began each time, "with the penalty of death in the electric chair."

The new date set for the executions was swift: Ed Ware, Alf Banks, Joe Fox, Albert Giles, John Martin, and Will Wordlow were sentenced to die July 23, one by one, beginning at sunrise. In the meantime, they were taken by train back to the death house at The Walls to wait out the two months.

"We and our attorneys feel that the officials did not deal fairly with us," Ware told newspaper reporters. He was certain that they would not have been convicted if "prejudice was left aside . . . for we are innocent."

Scipio declared that the state had pretended to have trials. As quickly as the jurors dealt their vengeful verdicts, he appealed each one of the cases to the Arkansas Supreme Court, this time on the grounds of exclusion of Black people from the juries.

Even though they'd lost, Scipio had changed the tenor of the trials, and he felt confident that the cases had reached a turning point. He'd shown that whites had caused the violence in Hoop Spur, and he'd coaxed white witnesses to testify about it. Scipio would use these developments later when he brought the cases to higher courts.

Governor Brough weighed in, saying that he was certain the retrials had been conducted with "absolute justice." Still, he put the executions of the Ware men on hold—for now— which gave Scipio time to focus again on the Moore Six, who were languishing in the death-house cells.

Scipio filed an appeal to the U.S. Supreme Court, asking the court to review the Moore verdicts. But when the response from the justices came, it wasn't what Scipio wanted to hear. The court declined to review the verdicts, opening the way for the executions and leaving Scipio with no clear options for saving those six men.

The decision had an even bleaker effect on Colonel Murphy, who'd continued to assist Scipio despite his declining health. Murphy died that same day. Scipio was certain it was a broken heart that killed him "on the very hour" that the decision was announced.

Scipio's primary white ally was dead. The lives of twelve men now depended solely on Scipio's ingenuity, while the full force of the Arkansas legal system pushed against them. The entire state seemed to be screaming for them to die.

The Moore Six waited in jail for Governor Brough to decide when they'd be executed, while the Ware Six kept their hopes pinned on Scipio's appeal to the Arkansas Supreme Court. "All we can do is read the scriptures, pray to the Lord and sing, and time passes on," Ed Ware said.

Helena organizations pressured Brough to electrocute the Moore Six, demanding that he keep the Committee of Seven's promise to execute them. The leaders of civic groups including the American Legion, the Lions Club, and Rotary insisted that they'd prevented lynchings only because they'd been told the prisoners would soon be executed legally. But they were losing what little patience they had. If the men were spared, they warned, then lynchings would definitely follow.

The governor gave in. He declared that the Moore executions would take place before his term ended on January 12, 1921, which was less than two months away.

"Last Hope Gone for Six Negroes" blared the headline in the *Arkansas Gazette*. But Scipio didn't believe it. He composed a letter to the *Gazette*, the *Arkansas Democrat*, and other newspapers, explaining that opinions would shift when the public learned the truth about the torture. Even though white people in Helena were "still insisting on blood," Scipio believed that many of them would change their minds. He demanded that the Moore Six must remain alive until a court

Although Governor Brough (center) believed the trials had been fair, he put the Ware executions on hold.

ruled on his appeal for the Ware Six. In Scipio's mind, the cases were intertwined: If the Ware Six were found innocent, then the Moore Six must be, too. There could be no justice for the Moore men if they'd already been put to death.

Scipio checked the major Little Rock newspapers, and he wasn't surprised that they didn't publish his letter. But it looked like he'd gotten through to the *Arkansas Democrat.* "Let the courts function," the editors wrote, urging Governor Brough to slow down and not have anyone killed until Scipio's latest appeal had been decided.

The *Gazette* continued to stir up hate: "Law abiding citizens of Phillips County were promised prompt and rigid enforcement of the law in the case of these murderers."

Brough gave in again, but this time to Scipio. He decided to let the new governor, Thomas McRae, set the execution date for the Moore Six. That delayed things for a couple of months until McRae took office. But McRae had already made clear that he didn't plan to pardon anyone.

In December of 1920, the state supreme court gave the cases a boost. It agreed with Scipio's argument that jury selection for the Ware Six hadn't been fair. There would have to be yet another set of retrials. Could the governor let the Moore Six be killed after a ruling like that? Scipio didn't think so. All twelve men had been tried under the same circumstances. Scipio hurried to tell the prisoners that things were moving in their favor.

"I am pretty sure that execution in the [Moore] cases will be stayed pending the outcome of the trials in the six [Ware] cases just reversed," Scipio wrote to the NAACP. And he bragged a little, too. "I am selfish enough to be very proud of the reversal in the Elaine cases, for the reason that, on account of the sudden illness of Colonel Murphy, I had to try all of the cases . . . myself."

As 1920 ended, the Elaine Twelve remained in the death house at The Walls, but their future looked a little less bleak. They didn't have their freedom, but they all had hope.

CHAPTER

Winter 1921

A fter Colonel Murphy died, his law partner, Edgar McHaney, filled in, but he annoyed Scipio and the NAACP by complaining about his pay. The NAACP gave McHaney only some of the money he demanded, but they still didn't seem to trust that a Black attorney like Scipio was capable of leading the cases. So they kept McHaney on the job.

The Moore Six stayed on death row, but McRae, the new governor, avoided setting an execution date. Scipio fought on with his usual "bull-dog tenacity" to prepare for the second retrials of the Ware Six. If he could win that case before McRae made a decision, Scipio could press the governor to pardon the Moore Six. But he knew that McRae might order their deaths at any time.

Scipio leaned on Judge Jackson to move the new retrials for the Ware Six out of Helena. The men hadn't received fair trials there, and he was sure they wouldn't this time either. Scipio also worried about their safety; the situation in Helena was so hostile he feared that they'd be kidnapped from the jail and killed during their retrials. "Any place is preferable to Helena," he stressed.

Both Judge Jackson and Scipio also knew that when the truth about the first Ware trials was told in a higher court, the men were likely to be found innocent. The judge was afraid that would cast doubts on the Moore verdicts, too, and he wanted to make sure the Moore Six had already been killed so the "solemn promise" was fulfilled.

With the pressure and the workload growing, Scipio convinced the NAACP to hire another assistant, but the organization agreed to pay only half of the fee. They left it up to Scipio to raise the rest of the funds.

"I don't know where I can get the money," Scipio told the NAACP, "but your money will be matched, even if I have to pay every dollar of it myself."

Scipio also hired a detective to search for evidence that would help him defend the men. He was slowly going broke by spending his own money, but saving the lives of his clients had become the most important mission of Scipio's life. "These men should not and must not go to the electric chair if it can be prevented, and it can!" he wrote.

Scipio regularly visited the men at The Walls, where Joe Knox and Ed Ware led prayers and singing. He was pleased that

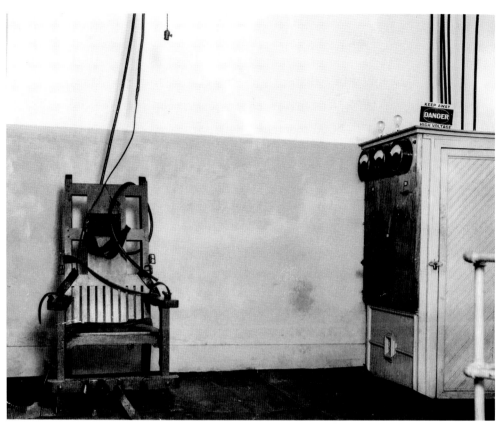

This electric chair at The Walls had the cruel nickname "Old Sparky."

the new warden—E. H. Dempsey—let the men out of their cells every day for exercise and gave them chores to help them stay fit. The Elaine Twelve also counseled younger inmates who weren't involved in their cases.

One of those young inmates was scheduled to be executed, and Knox and Ware spent time consoling him in the hours before his death. The man asked Knox and Ware to attend his execution.

Watching the man die in the electric chair shook up Knox and Ware badly. It was cruel timing. Later that day, Governor McRae alerted Knox and the rest of the Moore Six that they'd be put to death the same way on June 10.

The mood in Arkansas and across the country had grown worse in 1921. The white-supremacist group the Ku Klux Klan added 100,000 members that spring, and Black people were being lynched nationwide. Mobs swarmed jails in two Arkansas cities, seized two Black prisoners from their cells, and hanged them. Scipio worried even more that his clients would be taken from jail and lynched, too.

The Black community spoke out, flooding Governor McRae with petitions demanding that he postpone the executions.

Unsure of what to do next, McRae asked prosecuting attorney John Miller to provide him with a summary of the cases. Miller wrote that the sharecroppers had revolted, and that any of them who'd been killed had deserved it. He added that if the Hoop Spur incident hadn't thwarted the share- croppers' uprising, "there would not have been a white man, woman or child left in that part of the county to tell the story of their death." He denied that anyone had been tortured. Judge Jackson warned that "no more promises will be made" to protect the prisoners if they weren't put to death.

Because of those lies, the governor concluded that the trials had been fair. But Scipio's thoughts were way ahead of Miller's or Jackson's. He knew that Miller's own words would show that he was lying. Miller had asked a defendant about the whippings in an earlier trial, never denying that they'd occurred. Scipio would use that truth to help him during the Ware retrials. But that wouldn't save the Moore Six.

On June 8—two days before the Moore executions—the Jubilee Chorus of Arkansas Baptist College visited The Walls for a prayer and song service. The service was supposed to put the men in the right mood to die. The men didn't see things that way. They didn't draw their faith from the prayer service, but from their attorney. As one of the men told a reporter, "Scipio Jones won't let us die."

Even Scipio might have doubted those words. He raced from the jail, passing the gruesome execution chamber, where "Old Sparky" sat ready to inflict the fatal shocks. Six wooden coffins awaited the bodies.

As a last-ditch effort, Scipio hurried to the federal court to present an appeal, but he was met with a shock of his own. The judge was away on an assignment and wouldn't be back until after the execution date had passed.

Scipio's strategies had kept the men alive for nearly two years, but it looked as if he was finally out of options. Six members of the Elaine Twelve were scheduled to die in less than 48 hours.

CHAPTER 8

On Friday morning, June 10, a Chicago newspaper grimly reported that the Moore Six had been executed in Little Rock. The article solemnly recounted some of the men's last words before they died.

The report was wrong. The men remained very much alive inside The Walls because Scipio had pulled off a magnificent move. It stretched the legal limits of another court and was almost certainly improper, but Scipio's brilliant ploy had gained the men a few more days of life.

The Arkansas attorney general was outraged at what Scipio had done. He demanded that the executions go ahead as planned. But Governor McRae recognized the bind Scipio had created. The Arkansas Supreme Court quickly decided that the electrocutions would have to wait.

"No imminent danger of execution," Scipio declared.

"What a counsel of madness!" wrote the editors of the *Arkansas Democrat*.

Here's what Scipio had accomplished: With the federal court closed because of the judge's absence, Scipio turned instead to the chancery court in Little Rock—presided over by Judge John Martineau. Chancery courts generally dealt with cases involving matters such as contracts, wills, and divorces. They had no power over criminal cases or executions. But Scipio knew that Martineau had once granted an order

Scipio, left, stands with the Moore Six at The Walls. Front row, from left: Joe Knox, Ed Coleman, Paul Hall. Back row, from left: Ed Hicks, Frank Hicks, Frank Moore.

Linotype operators of the *Chicago Defender* newspaper set headlines. The *Defender* ran this one as Scipio worked toward moving the cases to the U.S. Supreme Court.

Renew Hope in Case of Elaine Men

Little Rock, Ark., Sept. 2.—It has been announced that efforts would be made to obtain from the Supreme Court of the United States a writ of certiorari in behalf of six Arkansas farmers condemned to die on September 23 for their connection with the Arkansas riots of 1919. It is then contemplated applying to a federal court for a writ of habeas corpus.

It was for appealing to the governor of Arkansas in behalf of these men that Prof. Robert T. Kerlin was handed a resolution of dismissal by the board of visitors of the Virginia Military Institute, Lexington, Va.

Six others are to be tried at Marianna, Ark., in October.

General counsel for the condemned men said to a Defender reporter: "We have great confidence of victory in the final outcome if given proper assistance."

The cases have been lingering in the courts for over two years and, due to the unusual amount of prejudice that has attended them, citizens of both races have interested themselves in the fight for justice.

that caused an execution to be postponed. He'd been scolded by the state supreme court, which overruled his decision. But Judge Martineau was stubborn, and he was eager "to cut through anything that seemed to stand in the way of justice." He wasn't at all afraid of being reprimanded again. He also had a lot of respect for Scipio from past dealings in his court.

Martineau ordered E. H. Dempsey—the warden of the state penitentiary—not to carry out the executions. And he issued a writ of habeas corpus, forcing Dempsey to appear in his court on Friday at 2:00 p.m., and to bring the six Moore defendants with him. Dempsey would have to explain why the men were being held in his prison and why the warden had the authority to keep them there. (HAY-be-us COR-pus is a Latin term, and it boils down to a basic rule in the U.S.: The Habeas Corpus Act of 1867 allowed state prisoners to appeal their cases in federal courts for protection against illegal imprisonment.)

Arkansas Attorney General J. S. Utley fumed. He argued that Martineau had no authority to make a ruling like that. But Scipio knew that only a higher court could overrule Martineau's decision, even if it was wrong. The state supreme court held a brief hearing and decided that proper arguments would have to wait until after the weekend.

Scipio was certain that Martineau's order would never hold up in the higher court. But the Moore men had once again outlived their execution date. And Scipio had done more than halt the killings for a few days. By opening the door for the state supreme court to consider the habeas corpus ruling,

Scipio had moved another piece of his long-term strategy into place. He had his eye on the U.S. Supreme Court.

So it didn't matter much when the Arkansas Supreme Court threw out Judge Martineau's ruling. It *did* mean that Governor McRae could set a new date for the executions, but he didn't seem to be in any hurry to do that.

Scipio was well aware that in the decades after the habeas corpus act had become law, the U.S. Supreme Court worked to limit its effects. A federal judge could get involved only after all appeals at the state level had been exhausted. And even if the state courts had made errors, the federal courts had to honor those decisions. A prisoner could win a habeas corpus decision only if the state was found to have violated the Constitution, or if it could be proven that the state had lost jurisdiction. In other words, Scipio would have to show that the state of Arkansas had been so negligent in its actions that it had lost control over the case and no longer deserved to have authority over the Moore Six.

The U.S. Supreme Court had *never* ruled that a state had lost jurisdiction. But Scipio knew, from reviewing a 1915 decision, that the court had confirmed the possibility that a state *could* lose it. The justices ruled against the defendant in that murder case and determined that the trials had not been "dominated by a mob." But if the defense had been able to prove that mob interference occurred, and that the state hadn't provided "a corrective process," then the murder defendant might have won.

Scipio felt strongly that there had been no corrective

processes for the Elaine Twelve, which would have required the appeals courts and the state supreme court to carefully review each of the trials and seek new evidence. At every step of the way, the courts had relied on the same tainted evidence that had been gained by torture. The trials had been so hideously unfair at every level, that if ever there was a case to take all the way to the U.S. Supreme Court, this was it.

Both the Moore and the Ware cases moved forward. Judge Jackson surprisingly allowed the Ware retrials to be moved to Lee County, and to begin in October. Governor McRae set the Moore executions for September 23.

And then Scipio did the unimaginable: He reached out to the enemy and made an astonishing breakthrough. He found two witnesses so credible that their testimonies couldn't be disputed, and he convinced them to tell the truth. Not only had the two men been on the scene during the Hoop Spur rampage, but they'd also spent crucial time at the Helena jailhouse in the days after. But these men hadn't been prisoners. They were the ones who'd done the whippings!

enry Smiddy and TK Jones were part of the posse that massacred sharecroppers the day after the Hoop Spur incident. It is likely that the detective Scipio had hired made the first contacts with them, but their change of heart was because of Scipio's ability to convince people to tell the truth.

Smiddy and TK Jones told Scipio that they'd seen white men mistakenly killed by other whites, and how the mob torched the church and burned it to the ground to cover up any evidence that the union meeting had been under attack. "Benches were turned over, window lights broken out on all sides of the church, glass scattered all over the floor, women's and men's hats and coats scattered around all over the floor and every evidence of a stampede in the church house," Smiddy recalled.

Both men had heard the Committee of Seven promise that the sharecroppers would be put to death. TK Jones said he whipped at least two dozen men to make them confess to crimes they hadn't committed.

Smiddy said the only member of the Elaine Twelve who hadn't been tortured was Ed Coleman, who was so old and frail that the guards thought a whipping would kill him. Each of the others had been tortured repeatedly, and their words were used against them in the trials.

"So far as I know no negro made a voluntary statement that implicated any other negro in anything criminal," TK Jones recalled. "The feeling against them was so strong and so

The *Arkansas Democrat* identified this as the Hoop Spur church where the union meeting took place. Henry Smiddy and TK Jones told Scipio that the mob had burned it to the ground.

universal that it was absolutely unanimous and no man could have sat upon a jury in any of these cases and have voted for acquittal and remained in Helena afterwards."

As Scipio listened to the two men, he knew that their lives would be in danger if they testified in court. Smiddy had been a deputy sheriff in Helena and now worked for the Missouri Pacific Railroad, where TK Jones was a supervisor. The mob would turn against them as swiftly and violently as they'd attacked the sharecroppers.

Both men insisted on telling the truth, and they handed Scipio their written confessions. They were soon fired from

Many sharecroppers were gunned down while they worked in fields like this one in the Arkansas delta.

their jobs, and law officers "began to make various charges against me for the sole purpose of compelling me to withdraw the affidavit," Smiddy said. Both men were arrested and jailed. Smiddy said his life was threatened.

Scipio bailed the men out and helped them flee from Arkansas. He spent at least $2,500 of his own money to help the men and their families over the next several months. They'd given him the written evidence he needed, and he built the next step of his strategy on that testimony.

Days before the new execution date for the Moore Six, McHaney—who had continued to whine about his pay—

abruptly quit after another dispute. The NAACP finally seemed to understand that Scipio had been carrying the load anyway, as one official remarked that "the colored lawyer seems to have been doing all the work, while the white lawyer has taken much of the money and left us at the crucial moment."

Scipio again filed a habeas corpus appeal, contending that the Moore Six were being held unlawfully at The Walls and that killing them would be a violation of their constitutional rights. He built his case that the Committee of Seven had "assumed and exercised the jurisdiction of the court by determining the guilt or innocence of those in jail." The committee had decided who would be imprisoned and sent to the electric chair, and the verdicts weren't reached in a fair trial, "but as part of the prearranged scheme." In other words, the court in Helena had yielded its jurisdiction over the trials to the Committee of Seven.

Scipio claimed that "the verdict of the jury was really a mob verdict." It was the first time he'd made this claim in court. Because of Smiddy and TK Jones, he had the evidence to prove it.

The judge ordered the state to respond to the charges, and Attorney General Utley again showed that he was no match for Scipio. He responded with a "demurrer," meaning that he believed the previous rulings from state courts should stand. But a demurrer also meant that the state was accepting Scipio's new arguments as facts and admitting that the testimonies of Smiddy and TK Jones were true. Utley simply believed that the new evidence didn't matter. He didn't care that hundreds of Black people had been massacred, that the Committee of Seven had promised that the Elaine Twelve would be executed, or that false confessions had been brought about by torture. But he didn't dispute that these things were true.

Even in the face of all that, the judge ruled that the convictions should stand. The Moore Six had lost again. But the judge permitted Scipio to make one last appeal to the U.S. Supreme Court. Utley's demurrer gave him what he needed to make his case "with the facts stated in our petition undenied."

Scipio had to write the new appeal while also preparing for the Ware retrials. By digging into his own savings and money raised by Black organizations, Scipio came up with $6,000 to hire attorneys to help with the Ware cases. That new opposition and the affidavits from Smiddy and TK Jones raised serious concerns for prosecutor John Miller, who asked Judge Jackson for a delay so he could try to strengthen his case. Jackson postponed the retrials to the spring of 1922.

Scipio had pulled off a double win over the state: The prosecution was obviously reluctant to retry the Ware Six, and the attorney general had agreed in the demurrer that the Moore Six trials had been tainted. Scipio's next move would be to prepare to appear before the U.S. Supreme Court. No Black attorney from Arkansas had ever argued a case in that court. Scipio Jones—born enslaved, self-taught, and relentless— was in line to be the first.

"The greatest case against peonage and mob law ever fought in the land, and involving 12 human lives, comes before the highest court!" proclaimed NAACP cofounder W. E. B. Du Bois.

ELAINE RIOTERS BEING RAILROADED, IS CHARGE

Former Bar Association Head Assails Arkansas for Sentences.

Washington, Jan. 9.—(By I. N. S.) —Appearing before the United States supreme court to plead for negroes condemned to die in connection with the Arkansas riots of 1919. Moorfield Storey, former president of American Bar Association, today charged the Arkansas courts, newspapers, leading citizens, Rotary club, American Legion and other organizations of Helena, Ark., with attempting to "railroad the negroes to death."

NAACP lawyer Moorfield Storey eagerly joined the defense team after reading Scipio's petition. In this clipping from the *Arkansas Democrat*, Storey said the local newspapers were trying to "railroad the negroes to death."

January 1923
Little Rock

The U.S. Supreme Court works slowly, so more than a year passed before the Moore Six hearing was scheduled. In the meantime, the state of Arkansas granted the prosecution two more postponements of the Ware retrials, leaving the lives of those six men in prison on hold, too. They were treated fairly well by the Lee County warden, which annoyed Judge Jackson. He ordered them back to the Helena jail, where they were dealt with more harshly.

Scipio prepared a flawless summary of the Moore cases for the U.S. Supreme Court. The NAACP's Walter White—who had previously been against Scipio's involvement—called it "one of the most human and thorough legal documents ever printed in America." But Scipio didn't expect to present the case alone. He asked the NAACP to find the best constitutional lawyer to participate, and officials tried to convince the organization's president, Moorfield Storey, to join the case. Storey was a highly respected civil rights attorney and had won two major cases in the Supreme Court.

Storey was reluctant to help with the Moore Six appeal. He claimed that he was too old and too busy, and that he hoped to retire soon. But the real reason was that he didn't think the case had a chance.

When Storey read Scipio's habeas corpus petition, he changed his mind completely. Scipio recounted how the peaceful gathering at the Hoop Spur church had been disrupted, how an angry mob had slaughtered innocent Black people in the aftermath, and how the rushed trials had been tainted by torture and a "bitterness beyond expression." The verdicts had been the verdicts of a mob, Scipio contended, so "the judgment against them is, therefore, a nullity."

Convinced, Storey declared that "it would be impossible to find a stronger case than the one which we have." He agreed to join Scipio's legal team.

Even with such a solid case, the outcome was very much in doubt. The Supreme Court, led by William Howard Taft, had not been supportive of civil rights. Taft had served one term as president of the United States after being elected in 1908. And after taking over as Chief Justice in 1921, he turned the Supreme Court in a more conservative direction.

Scipio objected when the NAACP asked attorney Ulysses S. Bratton to assist him and Storey, even though Scipio and

Bratton were friends. Only two defense attorneys were permitted to make arguments in a case before the Supreme Court. Scipio intended to be one of them. Was the NAACP squeezing him out in favor of the two white lawyers?

Bratton hadn't been involved since the earliest days of the ordeal, when Ed Ware hired his firm to negotiate cotton sales. But the NAACP believed that having a white attorney from Arkansas on the side of the defendants would provide "a splendid psychological effect" on the justices.

Scipio disagreed. He felt that Bratton's presence might backfire because it would anger prominent white people in Arkansas. No one had forgotten that Bratton advised the sharecroppers when their union was being formed, or that his son had been run out of town because of his own involvement.

In early 1923, the attorneys were told to be ready to appear before the Supreme Court during the third week of January. Scipio needed to make careful arrangements to travel to Washington, DC. He'd take a series of trains for the forty-four-hour trek—sitting upright because as a Black man he wouldn't be allowed into a sleeper car. He contacted the court's clerk on January 6 to confirm the date and couldn't believe the clerk's stunning reply. The case had been moved up on the schedule, and Scipio hadn't been told! He needed to be in Washington in twenty-four hours. Unless he grew wings, Scipio desperately needed forty-four.

Why hadn't the NAACP told him? Didn't they want him there? He'd led them to the highest court in the land. He'd composed one of the most convincing legal arguments in U.S. history.

But Scipio couldn't grow wings.

He rushed to the train station to see if the trip to DC was possible. But even if he could have hopped on a train that minute, the two-day trip would have been futile.

Ticket? Useless.

Telegram? Painful: "Don't expect to be able to be in Washington," Scipio wired the NAACP. "Depending on Mister Bratton and Judge Storey to appear."

So Scipio wasn't in court for *Moore v. Dempsey*—the most important case of his career—but his words were. Bratton and Storey relied heavily on Scipio's ideas and his research, recounting the massacre, the torture, the mobs, and the trials. Then Utley presented the state's familiar arguments, denying that anything had occurred in the way Scipio described. There'd been no massacre or torture, Utley claimed.

Chief Justice Taft—who many expected to side with the state—cut Utley off. "You demurred to the petition," he said, "thereby admitting the allegations." Taft was conservative, but he wasn't going to let Utley lie.

Utley fought back, but Taft and the other justices continued to challenge him. They also asked pointed questions of Bratton and Storey, but the defense attorneys left the court thinking they were likely to win.

Utley also expressed confidence. Despite his false arguments, states *did* have jurisdiction over murder cases. And the U.S. Supreme Court would be breaking precedent if it granted habeas corpus relief to state prisoners because they hadn't received fair trials. The future of American justice depended on the decision.

Moore v. Dempsey—Scipio's most famous case—
first reached the U.S. Supreme Court in 1921.

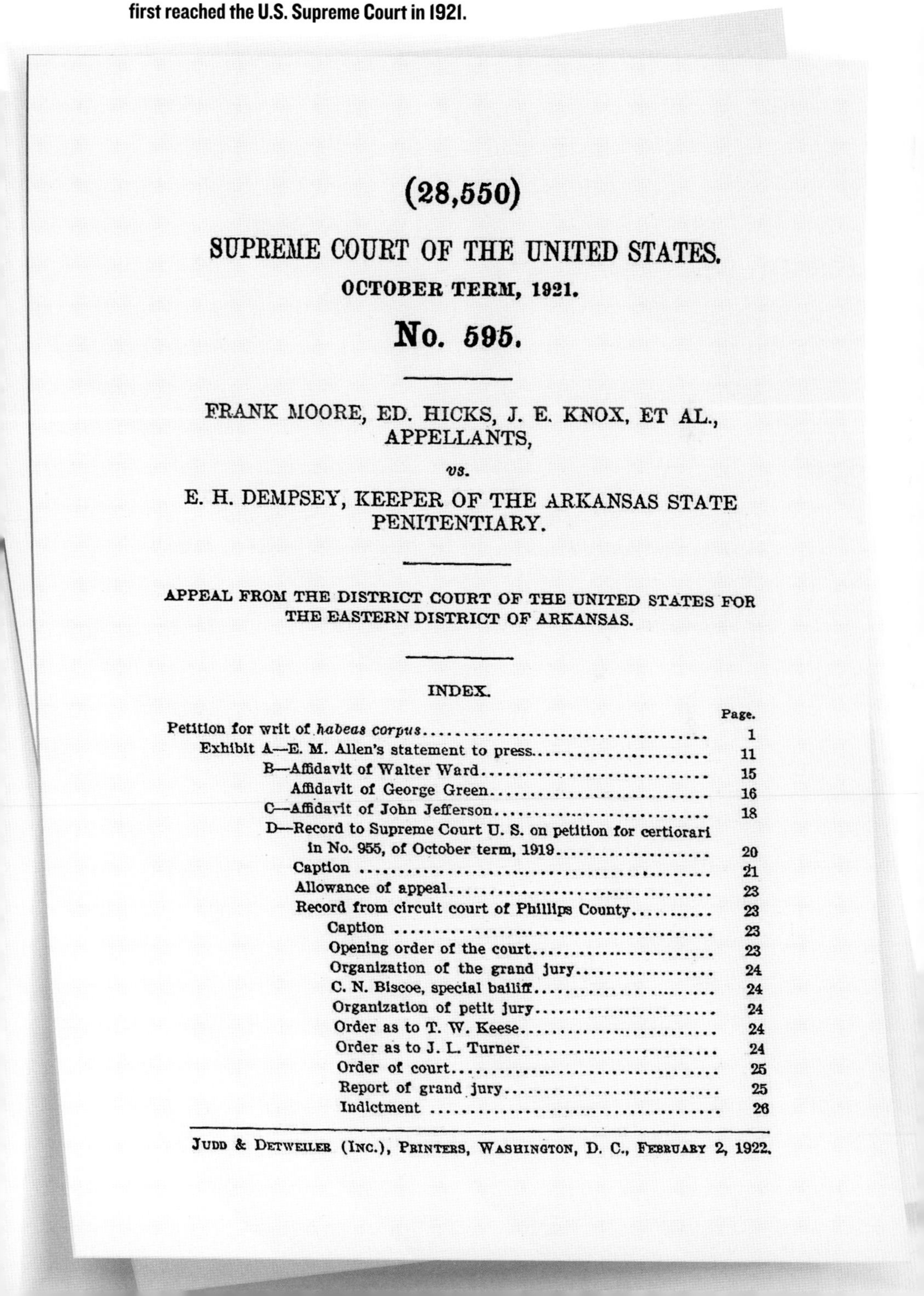

(28,550)

SUPREME COURT OF THE UNITED STATES.

OCTOBER TERM, 1921.

No. 595.

FRANK MOORE, ED. HICKS, J. E. KNOX, ET AL.,
APPELLANTS,

vs.

E. H. DEMPSEY, KEEPER OF THE ARKANSAS STATE
PENITENTIARY.

APPEAL FROM THE DISTRICT COURT OF THE UNITED STATES FOR
THE EASTERN DISTRICT OF ARKANSAS.

INDEX.

JUDD & DETWEILER (INC.), PRINTERS, WASHINGTON, D. C., FEBRUARY 2, 1922.

The U.S. Supreme Court in 1923. Front row, from left: Willis Van Devanter, Joseph McKenna, Chief Justice William Howard Taft, Oliver Wendell Holmes Jr., James C. McReynolds. Back row, from left: Pierce Butler, Louis Brandeis, George Sutherland, Edward Sanford. Sanford replaced a recently retired justice and had not yet been sworn in when the court heard *Moore v. Dempsey*, so that decision was made by eight justices.

Taft had a strong influence over the court's most conservative justices. He cast the first vote: in favor of the Moore Six. The majority agreed in a 6–2 vote, declaring that the state of Arkansas's corrective process "does not seem sufficient." The ruling meant that federal judges could overturn verdicts reached in a state court if the defendants had been denied their constitutional rights to due process.

The decision was monumental. W. E. B. Du Bois wrote that it was equal to any event since President Lincoln's Emancipation Proclamation. Not only did the decision pave the way for the Moore Six to be released, but Scipio's work had altered history. State courts could no longer get away with blatantly unfair trials and convictions. Black citizens had a pathway to challenge state rulings, and white supremacy would begin to crack.

Scipio's words had changed the court forever, but he wasn't rejoicing yet. The decision hadn't set the Moore Six free. The state had the opportunity to try them for murder yet again. And every one of the Elaine Twelve was still in prison.

Despite the biggest victory of his career, Scipio had a lot of work ahead.

Scipio worked tirelessly to keep the men alive. The cases cost him most of his own wealth.

CHAPTER 11

Spring 1923

S cipio knew how much words matter. Each time the prosecution requested delays of the Ware retrials, he responded by saying that the defendants were "ready for trial." He purposely did not agree to the delays.

In Arkansas, if a person charged with a crime remained in jail for two court terms without a trial and there was no good reason for the delay, they'd have to be set free. Prosecutor John Miller was incensed when Scipio made a motion to discharge the men because of this legality. The only reason the state had kept delaying the trials, Miller told the judge, was because he was waiting for key evidence and witnesses. But no new witnesses had been produced in the past three years.

Miller seemed to have no intention of going to trial but wanted the Ware men to rot in their jail cells instead. And as strong as the men were, after more than three years in jail the cruel and harsh treatment was wearing them down.

"Please Sir Help us if you can," Ed Ware wrote to Scipio. Ware had lost his health, sleeping on concrete cell floors and being shuttled from jail to jail. He explained how he and the men weren't allowed to "Walk on the ground and catch some fresh air." He needed relief from the suffering. Ware had witnessed the barbarity of dying in the electric chair. He needed out of jail.

Not surprisingly, the Lee County judge disagreed. He sided with Miller and denied Scipio's motion to release Ware and the five other sharecroppers.

Scipio appealed again to the Arkansas Supreme Court, and the judges agreed with him. "Justice delayed is justice denied," they wrote. Every person charged with a crime should have the right to a speedy trial and not suffer in jail for years without knowing their fate or defending their innocence.

Ed Ware, Alf Banks, Joe Fox, Albert Giles, John Martin, and Will Wordlow were nearly free. Incredibly, Miller still had the right to retry them, and the Arkansas court gave him two weeks to make up his mind. The Lee County judge ordered the sheriff to take the men to The Walls via train, but even that trip would be dangerous. A few months earlier, an angry white mob in Helena—looking for revenge because the Elaine sharecroppers were still alive—had brutally murdered a Black man named Will Turner in front of the Phillips County Courthouse. No one was arrested, charged, or tried for the lynching.

Now the *Helena World* newspaper was ready to stir up the hate against the Ware Six. Its headline proclaimed that the murderers of Helena lawmen had been set free.

Scipio waited anxiously at the Little Rock depot. The train carrying the men from Lee County rolled in, bringing with it a cloud of hissing steam. It was just after 11:00 p.m. on June 25, 1923. The moon was nearly full and shone brightly—unlike the sky over Hoop Spur four years earlier, in the fall of 1919, when Ed Ware drove to the little wooden church for the union meeting.

Nearby, Lula Ware and the other men's loved ones waited at the bottom of the hill below the penitentiary. Scipio had arranged for them to be there. They couldn't see the spot up the hill where Scipio and the sheriff arrived by convoy with the released prisoners, but the sounds would carry. They'd hear the commotion of the gathering crowd. And even though they were itching to race up that hill to the men they loved, they kept still.

For the Ware Six, it seemed like a miracle—stepping unshackled off the train, into a quiet sky and standing next to their attorney, Scipio Jones. The sheriff hurried to the prison gates to find the warden.

As a reporter rushed up to speak with him, Ed Ware knew he wasn't dreaming. He told the reporter that he felt "mighty fine." Photographs were snapped with Scipio and the men. Fifteen minutes went by. Forty-five. Then an hour. Finally, just past midnight, the sheriff came back and, without a word, shook hands with the night watchman and climbed into a taxi, leaving the men behind.

Scipio, left, and the Ware Six at The Walls. Front row, from left: Joe Fox, Albert Giles, Will Wordlow. Back row, from left: Alf Banks, John Martin, Ed Ware.

Were they really free after nearly four years of sleeping on cold floors, four years of few visitors, no friends, and food they could barely eat? What about the two-week wait? Maybe this was a setup and they'd be shot and killed if they walked away. Gazing up at the rifle-toting guards in the watchtower, nobody moved out of fear that the guards would shoot.

As Scipio had hoped, the warden had refused to accept the men as prisoners. That's why he'd brought the families here in the first place and why he had promised to keep the men under his care until the two weeks were up.

Finally, the night watchman shouted into the moonlight, "You're free to go!"

Ed Ware had waited forty-four months to hear those words. But he wouldn't sprint. Slowly, he made his way down the hill, walking backward with the others—not running, even though they longed to—but stepping calmly over the grass until they were out of shooting range. When they spotted their families at the bottom of the hill, the chorus of happy hollers started ringing.

Astonished voices pierced the new morning with joyous cries. "You never heard such shouting and singing and praising the Lord in your life," a reporter wrote.

Scipio had once again accomplished the impossible. He'd saved six lives from certain death. He'd negotiated with people who knew right from wrong yet were governed by hate. But what really mattered was the scene in front of him: the joyful reunion of six brave and innocent men, sentenced to die but now free and in the loving arms of their families.

The Ware men were officially free, but they'd never set foot in Hoop Spur again. Scipio had made arrangements for most of them to relocate to northern cities like Chicago, where they'd be safer.

Scipio couldn't rest on his victories. Other innocent men were still in jail. Namely, the Moore Six, whose lives ticked away at The Walls. Yes, they'd won the landmark Supreme Court case, but that didn't mean they were free.

The six men spent their days inside the death house or doing manual labor. Even eighty-two-year-old Ed Coleman, the oldest Arkansan ever on death row, endured back-breaking work in the prison fields. This was only going to change if Scipio found a way to get them released.

The yard inside The Walls. Guards with loaded rifles stood ready in the watchtower.

As part of the *Moore v. Dempsey* decision, the U.S. Supreme Court had ruled that the state must hold a hearing. Scipio would again have to prove that the Moore trials had been unfair—the outcome predetermined by an angry mob of white citizens. If he won, the Moore men would be free. If he didn't, they would be executed.

Based on the evidence, winning the court hearing looked like a lock for Scipio. But many white Helena residents were outraged that the Ware Six had been released. "They have simply gotten their freedom through the failure of the state to bring them to trials," a newspaper claimed. Killing the Moore Six remained a priority.

Scipio knew that the prosecution had no reliable witnesses. And the two lawmen the prosecution had relied on in the November 1919 trials—and whose lies had sealed the fate of the Moore men—were now key witnesses for the defense. Scipio had those sworn testimonies from TK Jones and Henry F. Smiddy about their roles in the massacre and the torture. After years of lying, their guilt had prompted a change. "I did what I did for the Colored People in the South," Smiddy wrote. "I knew the streight of the thing and wanted to see them come out of it."

Even with the truth on his side, Scipio hoped to avoid a hearing. While TK and Smiddy had been brave enough to own up to what they'd done, their fears might keep them from testifying in court. "They want to get me back down their to kill me," Smiddy wrote, referring to white residents of Helena who'd been promised that the sharecroppers would be executed.

Smiddy hadn't set foot in Arkansas since signing his statement. Hiding out in Topeka, Kansas, he wrote that he'd been "forced to leave on account of the affidavit I made for HON Scipio Jones."

Even if Smiddy and TK *would* risk their lives and take the stand at the hearing, Scipio had another reason not to put them there. The men had lost their jobs and were penniless, so he and the NAACP paid their rent and grocery bills. In a court of law it would look like a bribe; it would appear that the men had been paid to make their confessions.

Scipio could only avoid a hearing if the prosecution agreed and the governor set the men free. He suspected that the prosecution didn't want a hearing either. And in a "strictly confidential" letter to Scipio, attorney John Miller indicated that the state wanted to be done with the cases. It wasn't because the prosecutors cared about the fate of the sharecroppers or admitted that they were innocent. It was because they truly didn't have any honest witnesses. TK Jones and Smiddy had provided Scipio with the names of every Helena resident who'd tortured the prisoners. But before a deal to release the men could be made, the leaders of Phillips County had to agree to it.

Scipio explained all of this to the NAACP. "Do you think it would be advisable," he asked, to accept "short prison sentences for our Elaine clients?"

Astonishingly, NAACP officials wrote back that they didn't want a compromise that might appear to diminish "the very great moral victory which has been won" in the Supreme Court.

"Even if we lost them and the men were sentenced or executed it would not hurt our record in the fight at all," wrote one NAACP official.

Scipio's sole aim was to free the men, but the NAACP seemed more intent on continuing the fight—even if the six men were killed!

Scipio wouldn't wait any longer. This was his case, and he took that responsibility very seriously. He had to move quickly to avoid a hearing and other potential disasters. It would be dangerous for him to set foot in Helena again. The last time he'd been there, in May of 1920, he'd had to keep his lodging secret. But six lives were at stake, so Scipio risked personal danger again and boarded a train to Helena.

Scipio knocked on the doors of Helena community leaders and asked them to sign a petition urging a "full and complete pardon" of the Moore Six. Since there was no evidence that the sharecroppers committed any crime, "it would be fair and right, and in keeping with justice" if they were freed.

More than one hundred people signed the petition. After Scipio returned to Little Rock, he personally delivered it to Governor McRae.

Remarkably, the Committee of Seven—the group that had spread false stories of an insurrection, indicted the sharecroppers, and orchestrated the sham trials after promising that the men would be executed—now signed their own petition. It requested that the Moore men be freed, but under different terms—terms that would save the reputation of the plantation owners and other leaders who formed the committee. The sharecroppers were guilty, the Committee of Seven insisted, but to keep trying them in court would be too big a burden on the county. They asked McRae to change the sentences from first-degree murder to second-degree murder and to twelve-year sentences in the state penitentiary. If Scipio and the governor agreed, it meant that the Moore Six had already served a third of their sentences. They could be released for serving that much time.

"I hesitate to assume the responsibility of turning down an offer," Scipio wrote to the NAACP, knowing how it would "save the lives of 6 men and in a short time will release them from further imprisonment."

By early November 1923, Scipio had negotiated a deal. The Moore men would plead Not Guilty and McRae would shorten their sentences to twelve years—the penalty for second-degree murder—and promise to release them within twelve months. He'd also free fifteen other Elaine sharecroppers who were still serving terms for lesser convictions at the Cummins State

Prison Farm. In return, Scipio and the Moore men would waive their right to a hearing, which they didn't want anyway.

The men wouldn't be pardoned; they'd receive indefinite furloughs. That compromise would help the Committee of Seven save face. If Scipio had to accept that as part of the deal, so be it. Within a year, the Moore men would be free.

Governor McRae agreed to all of it, saying that he'd done so only because the Committee of Seven asked him to.

Six months later, in May 1924, McRae released some of the sharecroppers from the Cummins prison farm but none of the Moore Six. By the fall he'd announced that no one would receive furloughs during the harvest—not even Ed Coleman, who was now eighty-three—until the prison's crops were hauled in.

As the one-year mark of the deal Scipio had brokered came and went in November, he grew suspicious. In December, McRae dropped this bombshell news: The Moore Six would "not receive clemency."

McRae had lied. He'd reneged on the deal he'd agreed to. To make matters worse, he'd soon be out of office. And like Governor Brough before him, McRae left the fate of the Moore men in the hands of the incoming governor.

While Scipio fumed, he didn't criticize the governor. He knew he had to find a way to change McRae's mind. The incoming governor had been elected with the backing of the Ku Klux Klan, and he'd promised that his first action in office would be to electrocute the Moore Six. Scipio had three weeks to convince McRae to pardon the men, or they would surely die.

13

December 1924

S cipio had spent five years racing against time to save twelve innocent men from wrongful deaths. He'd lost his fortune because of it. The Cadillac and chauffeur were long gone, and so were his rental properties. Scipio confided to the NAACP that he was a "financial wreck." And he hadn't anticipated Governor McRae's latest deception.

Perhaps because of this monumental breach of trust, combined with Scipio's round-the-clock dedication to saving the Moore men, his health was failing. He couldn't get rid of a nasty cough. December had been cold in Little Rock and he hadn't been heating his house much. Every spare dime had gone into saving the lives of the men, and he wasn't about to give up on them now.

Scipio had run out of appeals. He couldn't go to the U.S. Supreme Court again. He typed up a new petition and boarded another train to Helena, where he collected signatures from Helena town leaders for a full and complete pardon of the Moore Six.

Scipio didn't take any chances. He also visited leaders in Elaine and had them sign the petition. Within four days in Phillips County, he'd collected close to eight hundred signatures. Even the county's most notorious prosecutor and Scipio's nemesis, John Miller, was now asking the governor to release the men.

Arriving safely back in Little Rock on December 24—Christmas Eve—Scipio knocked on the door of the governor's mansion and handed McRae the petition. By then, Scipio was battling such a high fever that he was shivering, and he struggled to make his way home. The Christmas before he'd gone to the warm, firelit house of his friends, who'd shared with him their meal of oyster stew, sausages, and eggs. This year, Scipio trudged home and fell into a deep sleep.

One week passed, then two weeks, with no word from the governor. Everyone knew that January 14 was the final day that McRae would be in office. On the morning of January 13, Scipio—still weak from illness—forced himself out of bed, faced the wind, and made his way to the governor's mansion to offer his final plea for the Moore men. In his usual manner, Scipio would have rested his hat on his lap, adjusted his gold pocket watch, and calmly stated his case.

After the meeting, Scipio—always the optimist—wired a telegram to the NAACP with these five words: "Anticipate favorable results by tomorrow."

Could McRae be trusted this time? Scipio had to believe. He'd done all he could legally, financially, and morally for the Moore Six. Their lives were in the hands of the governor.

Late that afternoon, McRae completed his last act as governor. He granted the Moore men indefinite furloughs.

Governor Thomas McRae said he wouldn't pardon any of the Elaine Twelve men.

They hadn't been pardoned, but they were free! And that's what mattered. There was so much jubilation at the Washington headquarters of the NAACP that they forgot to send Scipio a telegram of thanks.

First thing the next morning, clutching the signed document, Scipio arrived at The Walls to pick up the Moore men. Loading their worn and featherlight suitcases into taxi cabs didn't take long. As Frank Moore, brothers Ed and Frank Hicks, Preacher Joe Knox, Paul Hall, and Ed Coleman were driven away as free men, they passed a haunting sight. Strewn across the prison yard were wooden coffins meant for their burials but now warped and unused.

Every sharecropper—seventy-five of them imprisoned

because they'd attended a union meeting at Hoop Spur and twelve more condemned to die by electrocution—had lived. Despite the "cauldron of hate" and the corruption and the lies, Scipio Africanus Jones had changed everything. He'd utilized the truth and the law and his persuasive powers to save the lives of twelve innocent men. He'd brought their voices to the highest court in the land. There, he'd made the Constitution live up to its promise. He'd spent his fortune on freedom, and freedom had been delivered.

"All Hail Judge Jones," a newspaper proclaimed. "Praise him for his knowledge of law, his nerve, his patience and his sagacity."

Scipio Africanus Jones in 1924

EPILOGUE

"There are no cowards among us— no slackers on our rolls." —SCIPIO JONES

oore v. Dempsey was the first U.S. Supreme Court ruling in favor of Black defendants in a criminal case. It set a legal precedent that ensured the protection of defendants' constitutional rights and changed American law by holding state courts accountable, thanks to Scipio Jones. By creating a legal path to the U.S. Supreme Court that ensured the integrity of the Fourteenth Amendment, *Moore v. Dempsey* crushed a half century of court cases ignoring and brutalizing its meaning. For decades after, civil rights cases relied on this historic Supreme Court decision to defend constitutional rights.

The NAACP summed it up (eventually) in its high praise of Scipio, proclaiming that he had "rendered a service not

This flag was displayed outside the NAACP offices in New York City to call attention to the frequency of lynchings in the United States. The photo was taken in 1936; it wasn't until 2020 that an anti-lynching bill was passed by the U.S. House of Representatives.

STOP LYNCHING
N.A.A.C.P.
BUILD DEMOCRACY

A MAN WAS LYNCHED YESTERDAY

only to the men whose lives were saved and who were freed from prison," but that he'd also "benefitted all America."

Scipio never stopped fighting for racial equality and justice after *Moore v. Dempsey*. He worked against systemic racism in America's prisons and stood up to Arkansas law schools who barred Blacks from enrolling by convincing the state legislature to fund educational opportunities for law students of color.

While he and Walter White never became friends, Scipio continued to work with the NAACP, where he was celebrated after freeing the Elaine Twelve men. He became a lifelong member and championed the civil rights organization, speaking on its behalf. The NAACP's Legal Defense Fund team remains a powerful force for social justice today. Its legal legacy began with Scipio Jones and *Moore v. Dempsey*.

Scipio's last major legal case, at the age of seventy-nine, was against the Little Rock school district. He sued to ensure equal pay for Black teachers and administrators, but he died in 1943, before the case was finished. There was, however, a young attorney working on the case with him. His name was Thurgood Marshall. The future U.S. Supreme Court justice and the first African American judge appointed to the highest court in the land always referred to Scipio as Judge Jones. Marshall completed the work that Scipio had championed by winning equal pay, and then legally ending school segregation with *Brown v. Board of Education*.

Not much is known about the lives of the Elaine Twelve men after they were finally released from jail. Scipio arranged for most of them to relocate to cities in the North. Some changed their names for protection because vengeful people still wanted them killed.

Many of these men "believed their lives were still in peril after being released from jail," said Dr. Brian Mitchell, a professor of history at the University of Arkansas at Little Rock. "Very few of them stayed in Arkansas. Most of them fled."

In 2018, nearly a century after the Elaine Massacre, Mitchell and a group of students began extensive research about the men's lives after leaving Arkansas.

Dr. Mitchell's team found graves for six of the men, two of them in Little Rock. U.S. Army veteran Frank Moore is buried in Little Rock's National Cemetery with the military honors he deserved; once released from prison he had found safety in Chicago working as a night watchman. Joe Knox followed Scipio to Little Rock and officially became a Baptist minister. Like Scipio, he's buried in the Haven of Rest Cemetery in Little Rock.

The team found other graves in Kansas, Illinois, Ohio, and Missouri, including Ed Ware and his wife, Lula, who are buried side by side in St. Louis. Ida B. Wells-Barnett reported that Ed Ware visited her in Chicago shortly after his release to thank her for inspiring the men when she visited them at The Walls.

Albert Giles ran a Chicago speakeasy that sold alcohol illegally during Prohibition. He died in 1937 from an injury after an altercation.

Alf Banks worked as a custodian and a steel company laborer in St. Louis until his death in 1941.

The oldest of the Elaine Twelve men, Ed Coleman, moved

to Memphis, Tennessee. He died in 1928 in his eighty-seventh year and is buried in Herbert, Arkansas.

"We believe the missing ones may have used fake names for the remainder of their lives," Dr. Mitchell said.

The men and women who set *Moore v. Dempsey* in motion by resisting subjugation and demanding economic power by unionizing in 1919 paid dearly. Many Black people lost their lives while being terrorized by white southerners in the Elaine Massacre, one of the deadliest mass lynchings of African Americans in history. In 2015, the Equal Justice Initiative documented 237 deaths of Black Americans in the massacre, although the full count will never be known and unmarked mass graves are yet to be confirmed. The EJI traced more than four thousand lynchings throughout the United States. Phillips County, Arkansas, where Elaine is located, had nearly five times as many victims as the county with the second highest total. No one has ever been charged with the murders of Black Arkansans who died in the massacre. After more than two hundred attempts throughout history, the U.S. Congress continually failed to pass a law to make lynching a federal crime. Finally, in February 2020, the House of Representatives passed the Emmett Till Antilynching Act.

It wasn't until many decades after the Elaine tragedy that historians began referring to the atrocity as a massacre instead of a race riot, acknowledging that killing hundreds of Black people and blaming the murders on a race riot was a lie. The number of white deaths was five, three of them likely the result of misfiring by their own men.

Sharecroppers stood up for better pay for their cotton. Some paid for it with their lives.

The five white people killed were celebrated as heroes for maintaining white supremacy in Arkansas, but nothing acknowledged or commemorated the deaths of the hundreds of African Americans murdered in the massacre. In 2017, the Elaine Massacre Memorial Committee formed in hopes of changing that and bringing the true story to the forefront of Arkansas history.

On the one-hundredth anniversary of the tragedy, the committee unveiled a memorial just steps from the Phillips County Courthouse to honor the victims. U.S. District Judge Brian Miller is a committee member whose family suffered greatly in the massacre. His relatives were murdered along the same train route that Scipio Jones rode into Helena. Other relatives of the Elaine Twelve also attended the ceremony, and most knew very little about how their sharecropper ancestors had stood up to white supremacy, or the price they paid for their stance.

Scipio Jones has remained largely unknown since he passed away in 1943. His funeral was held at the Bethel AME Church in Little Rock, where he'd been a member for more than fifty years. The city was still officially segregated back then, but Scipio's funeral was attended by both Black and white Arkansans, and the day was written about in many newspapers. He'd gained great respect in Little Rock, but only modest possessions. Yet he had everything he needed. He'd risked everything for the "life and death struggle" to fight for the rights of Black Americans, and he won. He'd been a single father and widower, and his heart had been broken by the early death of his only child, Hazel. But Scipio had three grandchildren (one of them named Scipio), and he eventually remarried, too. He owned the house that he lived in with his second wife, Lillie, and the furnishings in his law office, including his oak rolltop desk and thirty-five oak bookcases filled with his impressive collection of law books.

He also still had his gold pocket watch.

STATE OF ARKANSAS,
County of Pulaski. } ss.

IN THE PROBATE COURT OF SAID COUNTY

Administration on the Estate of __Lillie M. Jones__ _____ here applying for letters of

____Scipio A. Jones____

late of said County, being first duly sworn, deposes and says that the said____

____Scipio A. Jones____

_____ departed this life in __Little Rock, Pulaski County__

on or about the __28th__ day of __March__ _____ A. D. 19 __43__.

That the said____Scipio A. Jones_____

That, to the best of __my__ _____ knowledge and belief, the value of the Estate of the Deceased _____ died intestate.

is about the sum of__One Thousand_____ Dollars.

That the names and residence of the Heirs of the Deceased are as follows, viz:

Age

Lillie M. Jones (widow) _____ Residence at __Little Rock, Arkansas.__

Scipio A. Dowing (grandson) Residence at __Chicago, Ill.__

John E. Dowing (grandson). Residence at _____

Hazel Dowing Miller (granddaughter) Residence at __Vicksburg, Miss.__

_____ Residence at _____

_____ Residence at _____

AND FURTHER deposes and says that __she__ will make perfect inventory of and faithfully administer, all and singular, the goods and chattels, rights and credits of the Deceased, and pay __his__ debts, as far as the Assets which come to __her__ hands will extend, and the law direct; and that __she__ will account for, and pay over, according to law, all Assets which shall come to __her__ _____ hands or possession, so help __her__ God.

Lillie M. Jones

Subscribed and sworn to before me_____
this __11__ day of_____

PERSONAL PROPERTY		VALUE	
One flattop oak desk with adational glass top, 7 drawers		30	00
One oak typewriter desk with three drawers		25	00
One Royal Typewriter - 10A5679		40	00
Two 4-drawer oak filing cabinets	$25.00 ea.	50	00
Thirty-five (35) Book-case units	$5.00 ea.	175	00
Seven (7) bottoms, and 7 tops for bookcase units	$2.50 ea.	35	00
One 5½ ft oak library table with drawers		20	00
Six (6) oak office chairs, one of which swivel,		22	50
One gold watch		50	00
One iron Cary Safe		50	00
Law Library complete		1000	00
		(497	50

Scipio's list of possessions was
modest at the time of his death.

AUTHORS' NOTE

We first learned about Scipio Jones while researching a landmark case that occurred more than forty years after *Moore v. Dempsey*. Anxious to find out who Frank Moore was and the attorney representing him, we uncovered the chilling account of the Elaine Twelve men.

Our intention, at first, was to focus solely on the sharecroppers, the atrocities they endured, and the travesty of justice within the context of the Red Summer—the 1919 bloody trail across America and the fight for racial and economic equality. But the scope of that story seemed too vast and focused on violence. The more we read about attorney Scipio Jones and realized the magnitude of his actions to save the men and his own freedom struggle, we knew we had to focus on Scipio in order to tell the Elaine Twelve story.

One hundred years after the Elaine Massacre, we were surprised that no one had written a book for teenagers about Scipio Jones or the Elaine Twelve men. But American history is ugly. That doesn't mean it's to be avoided or that young readers shouldn't learn about it until they're adults. We wrote about this history to hold it accountable. We told it so that it won't be forgotten, so the victims and survivors aren't erased but heard. We also wrote this book to leave a record that can help ensure that it doesn't happen again. And we focused on the people who stood up to the ugliness, the domestic terrorism inflicted on Black citizens, the judicial injustice—and won.

This is also a story about hope, determination, tenacity, and fighting back. In this case, we see these important qualities illustrated through Scipio's expert interpretation of state and constitutional law, through testimony by the men of their innocence and the torture they endured, and through the affidavits of two perpetrators whom Scipio convinced to denounce white supremacy and confess in time to ensure their victims' freedom.

This is a story about Black Americans standing up for their constitutional rights in the early 1900s and succeeding at holding democracy accountable—something that we've failed to let our young people know and read about. And they did this amidst segregation, violence, white supremacy, and the horror and brutality of lynching.

We couldn't succeed in telling Scipio's story and the story

of the Elaine Twelve men without first knowing who Scipio was as a person. Yet Scipio didn't write an autobiography or any account of his more than five-year fight to save the lives of these innocent sharecroppers. (He had proposed such a book to the NAACP, but Walter White rejected it, and Scipio dropped the idea.)

We began to discover who Scipio was through snippets of information. We isolated all of his words found in letters, telegrams, documents, and court transcripts. We highlighted all pertinent correspondence to him, newspaper and magazine articles written about him, and every oral history collected on Scipio told by colleagues and friends. As we assembled all this information and interpreted it, these varied sources of information showed us who Scipio Jones was as a person and attorney. It became clear what he stood for and the depths of his commitment to save the Elaine Twelve men from electrocution.

It might take one hundred years, but the truth always rises when you search for it—in a sentence or quotation, even in a biased newspaper; in interviews and confessions or in American Legion minute books. Even in death Scipio showed us his convictions. By tracing how all the wealth he'd accumulated during his career had been spent to support and save the sharecroppers and their families—leaving him with a few pieces of office furniture, some law books, and his beloved pocket watch—we could write about the many ways Scipio did all he could for justice.

We are grateful to historian Tom Dillard for his invaluable collection at the Butler Center for Arkansas Studies in Little

Rock, where we dived into the pivotal research on Scipio that he has amassed since the 1970s. Dillard collected oral histories from people who knew and worked with Scipio and are no longer alive; he recorded their recollections simply and clearly on index cards—proof that oral histories need not be elaborate.

Also at the Butler Center, we delved into the comprehensive research materials assembled by attorney Grif Stockley for his books and other works.

To learn about Scipio's relationship with the NAACP and his tireless work on *Moore v. Dempsey*, we read NAACP telegrams, papers, and letters. Many of these actual items had been lost, but because of the foresight of historian and activist Arthur I. Waskow, we had his papers to refer to. Most fortunately, Waskow had transcribed much of the information from the NAACP files on typewritten pages before it disappeared. This proved invaluable in discovering direct evidence of Scipio's hard work, his hopes of becoming the first Black attorney to defend a criminal case in the U.S. Supreme Court, and his frustrations with the NAACP.

The writings of activist–journalist Ida B. Wells-Barnett brought depth and understanding to us about the lives of the sharecroppers. Since Wells-Barnett had condemned lynchings in her newspaper articles for years, her life had been threatened in the South. She'd moved to Chicago but again risked death by traveling to Arkansas to visit the men at The Walls, where she gained their trust. She chronicled their lives and their testimonies, creating the first primary source and only published account by a journalist at the time that told of the sharecroppers' personal lives, their eyewitness accounts of the massacre, and its aftermath.

Another obstacle we faced in researching information and sources for our book was the credit given to white attorneys for the criminal cases Scipio was responsible for, including the decision the U.S. Supreme Court handed down in the pivotal *Moore v. Dempsey* case. As we researched segregation customs in the South, we realized that Black attorneys needed white attorneys as colleagues to set up a ruse in order to successfully practice criminal law in the early twentieth century. So, with every proceeding we asked ourselves, *"Where was Scipio Jones?"* Letters, telegrams, briefs, and transcripts always told us. Reading the trial records of *Moore v. Dempsey* and the letters Moorfield Storey wrote to the NAACP on why he agreed to argue the case in the Supreme Court, it became clear that Scipio's work not only formed the foundation of the argument, but the argument itself. And there was no way that we were going to have history continue to ignore Scipio Jones and not give him credit for so much litigation, and for preparing the brief and being responsible for the landmark *Moore v. Dempsey* case.

As we delved into the court proceedings and the many electrocution postponements Scipio secured for the share-croppers, it became difficult for us to keep track of storylines, especially once the men were divided into two separate cases. To make this manageable to write about, we created not only multiple timelines that could be superimposed for accuracy and keep our story sequential and moving, but also judicial timelines complete with (we hope) easy-to-understand explanations and terms that brought clarity to the proceedings and punctured complicated, legal language. For this we thank the Honorable Patricia Whalen, who has spent most of her professional life seeking justice for victims of people who abuse their power. From international judge of the War Crimes Chamber of Bosnia and Herzegovina to drafting laws at the Hague Convention, Judge Whalen is known for bringing clarity and context to various courts of law. We're so grateful to her for critiquing our manuscript and answering our many questions that began with, "Does *this* really mean *this?*"

Finally, we'd like to thank our editor, Carolyn Yoder, for patiently waiting the three years we took to research and write this story and for always being steadfast in publishing civil rights stories that most editors would turn down.

Scipio's granddaughter Hazel Adams attended the dedication of the Scipio Jones Post Office Station in 2007.

In Little Rock, Arkansas, which Scipio Jones called home, the last house he owned is a national landmark, yet it's abandoned and overgrown with weeds, and no plaque is there to honor his place in history. However, two buildings were named after him: Little Rock's all-Black high school was renamed Scipio A. Jones High School in 1928. It closed in

This simple gravestone marks Scipio's final resting place in Little Rock.

the 1970s when school segregation officially ended in Arkansas, and it later burned down. A regional post office building is named the Scipio A. Jones Station. Yet when we visited there, people had no idea who Scipio was. And if you walk into the Haven of Rest Cemetery in Little Rock, you'll find, close to the paved pathway, a gray marble headstone covered in lichen, with these simple, boldly carved words:

SCIPIO A. JONES
ATTORNEY AT LAW

Many sharecroppers left Phillips County after the Elaine massacre.

BIBLIOGRAPHY

BOOKS

Bush, A. E. and P. L. Dorman, eds. *History of the Mosaic Templars of America*. Fayetteville, AR: University of Arkansas Press, 2008.

Coke, Octavius, ed. *The Scrapbook of Arkansas Literature*. American Caxton Society Press, 1939.

Cortner, Richard C. *A Mob Intent on Death: The NAACP and the Arkansas Riot Cases*. Middletown, CT: Wesleyan University Press, 1988.

Hanna, H. L., ed. *Transcripts of the Trials of [Albert] Giles & Joe Fox, John Martin & Alf Banks, Jr,. and Will Wordlow. Phillips County Courthouse, October, November 1919*. Harrisburg, AR: Aquila, 2016.

Lancaster, Guy, ed. *The Elaine Massacre and Arkansas*. Little Rock, AR: Butler Center Books, 2018.

McWhirter, Cameron. *Red Summer: The Summer of 1919 and the Awakening of Black America*. New York: Henry Holt and Company, 2011.

Ovington, Mary White. *Portraits in Color*. New York: Viking, 1927.

Ovington, Mary White, *The Walls Came Tumbling Down*. Andesite Press, 2017.

Richardson, Clement. *The National Cyclopedia of the Colored Race*. Montgomery, AL: National Publishing Co., 1919.

Stockley, Grif. *Blood in Their Eyes: The Elaine Race Massacres of 1919*. Fayetteville, AR: University of Arkansas Press, 2001.

Stockley, Grif. *Ruled by Race: Black/White Relations in Arkansas from Slavery to the Present*. Fayetteville, AR: University of Arkansas Press, 2009.

Waskow, Arthur I. *From Race Riot to Sit-In, 1919 and the 1960s; A Study in the Connections Between Conflict and Violence*. Garden City, NY: Doubleday & Company, 1966.

Wells-Barnett, Ida B. *The Arkansas Race Riot*. Chicago, 1920.

Wells-Barnett, Ida B., and Alfreda M. Duster. *Crusade for Justice: The Autobiography of Ida B. Wells*. University of Chicago Press, 1972.

Whitaker, Robert. *On the Laps of Gods: The Red Summer of 1919 and the Struggle for Justice that Remade a Nation*. New York: Three Rivers Press, 2008.

White, Walter. *A Man Called White*. Athens, GA: University of Georgia Press, 1995.

Williams, Lee E., and Lee E. Williams II. *Anatomy of Four Race Riots: Racial Conflict in Knoxville, Elaine (Arkansas), Tulsa, and Chicago, 1919–1921*. University and College Press of Mississippi, 1972.

Woods. E. M., *Blue Book of Little Rock and Argenta, Arkansas*. Little Rock: Central Printing Company.

GOVERNMENT DOCUMENTS

In the United States District Court for the Western Division of the Eastern District of Arkansas. Frank Moore, Ed Hicks, J. E. Knox, Ed Coleman and Paul Hall Petitioners vs. E. H. Dempsey, Keeper of the Arkansas Penitentiary Defendant. Petition for a Writ of Habeas Corpus.

Pleas Before the Hon. J. M. Jackson, Judge of the First Judicial Circuit of the State of Arkansas, Phillips County, Arkansas, October Term, November 4th, 1919. State of Arkansas vs. #4481 Murder in the First Degree, Albert Giles and Joe Fox.

Pleas Before the Hon. J. M. Jackson, Judge of the First Judicial Circuit of the State of Arkansas, Phillips County, Arkansas, October Term, November 4th 1919. State of Arkansas vs. #4482 Murder in the First Degree, John Martin and Alf Banks, Jr.

Pleas Before the Hon. J. M. Jackson, Judge of the First Judicial Circuit of the State of Arkansas, Phillips County, Arkansas, October Term, November 4th, 1919. State of Arkansas vs. #4482 Murder in the First Degree, Will Wordlow.

Supreme Court of the United States, October term 1921. "Frank Moore, Ed Hicks, J. E. Knox, et al., appellants vs. E. H. Dempsey, Keeper of the Arkansas State Penitentiary."

PERIODICALS

Arkansas Gazette. "Scipio Jones, State Negro Leader, Dies." March 29, 1943.

Associated Press. "LR Post Office renamed for Former Slave-Turned-Lawyer." August 24, 2007.

Arkansas Democrat. "Scipio Jones Special Judge." April 8, 1915.

Chicago Defender. "Mobs Slay Arkansas Families."
October 11, 1919.

The Courier Index (Marianna, AR). "Eleven Elaine Rioters
Must Die in Electric Chair; 37 Must Serve Pen Sentences."
November 7, 1919.
———. "Negroes Planned Wholesale Murder of Whites on
Monday." October 10, 1919.
———. "Phillips County is Scene of Shocking Race Riots."
October 3, 1919.

The Crisis. "The Real Causes of Two Race Riots."
December 1919.

Desmarais, Ralph H. "Military Intelligence Reports on
Arkansas Riots: 1919–1920." *The Arkansas Historical
Quarterly,* Summer 1974.

Dillard, Tom. "Scipio A. Jones." *Arkansas Historical Quarterly,*
Autumn 1972.

Graves, John William. "Protectors or Perpetrators? White
Leadership in the Elaine Race Riots." *Arkansas Review,*
August 2001.

Helena World. "Convictions in the Insurrection Cases."
November 5, 1919.
———. "Convictions Now Number 65." November 7, 1919.
———. "Elaine Insurrection is Over; Committee of 7 in
Charge." October 3, 1919.
———. "Five Others Found Guilty." November 4, 1919.
———. "Frank Hicks Found Guilty of Lee's Murder."
November 3, 1919.
———. "O.R. Lilly Murdered by Negro Rioters in Elaine."
October 2, 1919.
———. "Six Negroes Found Guilty." November 4, 1919.
———. "Statement by Committee of 7." October 12, 1919.
———. "A Verdict in Six Minutes.' November 4, 1919.

Jennings, Jay. "12 Innocent Men." *The New York Times*, June 22, 2008.

Jones, Scipio. "The Arkansas Peons." *The Crisis*, December 1921.

Kilpatrick, Judith. "(Extra)ORDINARY MEN: African-American Lawyers and Civil Rights in Arkansas Before 1950." *Arkansas Law Review*, 2000.

Nichols, Ronnie A. "Conspirators or Victims? A Survey of Black Leadership in the Riots." *Arkansas Review*, August 2001.

Stockley, Grif and Jeannie M. Whayne. "Federal Troops and the Elaine Massacres: A Colloquy." *The Arkansas Historical Quarterly*, Autumn 2002.

Stockley, Griffin J. "The Legal Proceedings of the Arkansas Race Massacres of 1919 and the Evidence of the Plot to Kill Planters." *Arkansas Review*, August 2001.

Taylor, Kieran. "'We Have Just Begun': Black Organizing and White Response in the Arkansas Delta, 1919." *The Arkansas Historical Quarterly*, Autumn 1999.

Uenuma, Francine. "The Massacre of Black Sharecroppers that led the Supreme Court to Curb Racial Disparities of the Justice System." Smithsonian.com, August 2, 2018.

Waterman, John S. "The Aftermath of Moore V. Dempsey." *Washington University Law Review*, January 1933.

Whayne, Jeannie M. "Low Villains and Wickedness in High Places: Race and Class in the Elaine Riots." *Arkansas Review*, August 2001.
——. "Oil and Water: The Historiography of the Elaine Riots." *Arkansas Review*, August 2001.

ADDITIONAL SOURCES

Dillard, Tom W.: Black Arkansiana Collections, Butler Center for Arkansas Studies, Central Arkansas Library Systems, Little Rock, AR.

Ferguson, Bessie. "The Elaine Race Riot." Department of History thesis, Hendrix College, Conway, AR, August 1927.

"Inward Facts About Negro Insurrection," Committee of Seven statement to the press, October 7, 1919.

Jones, Scipio, et al., Brief for Appellants in the Supreme Court of Arkansas, 1920.

"Moore v. Dempsey," *Central Arkansas Library System (CALS) Encyclopedia of Arkansas History & Culture*: encyclopediaofarkansas.net/entries/moore-v-dempsey-5200/.

NAACP files of "Elaine Riot" copied by Arthur L. Waskow, Wisconsin State Historical Society Library, University of Wisconsin, Madison, WI.

Personal communication: Brian Mitchell to Rich Wallace, February 2019 and March 2020.

"Shadows of the Past: Dr. Brian Mitchell and Students Uncover Forgotten African American History in Arkansas," UALR.edu/orsp/2019/11/25/shadows-of-the-past, November 25, 2019.

Stockley, Grif, research materials at the Butler Center for Arkansas Studies, Central Arkansas Library Systems, Little Rock, AR.

"UA Little Rock Professor, Students Discover Locations of Missing Elaine 12 Graves," UALR.edu/news/2018/11/08 missing-elaine-12-graves, November 8, 2018.

PERSONAL VISITS

Arkansas Studies Institute, Little Rock, AR

Butler Center for Arkansas Studies, Little Rock, AR

Haven of Rest Cemetery, Little Rock, AR

Mosaic Templars Cultural Center, Little Rock, AR

Scipio Jones House, Little Rock, AR

United States Post Office, Scipio A. Jones Station, Little Rock, AR

FOR FURTHER INFORMATION

Elaine Massacre Memorial, Helena, AR
Website: elainemassacrememorial.org

"Elaine Race Massacre: Red Summer in Arkansas," University of Arkansas, Little Rock, online exhibit, UALRexhibits.org/elaine

Arkansas sharecroppers prepare for a day of work in the fields.

SOURCE NOTES

The source of each quotation in this book is indicated below. The citation provides the first words of the quotation and its document source. The sources are listed in the bibliography.

Page 7

"This is a life and . . .": Scipio Jones letter to Walter White, March 25, 1921, quoted in Whitaker, p. 237.

CHAPTER 1

"of which there were several": Scipio Jones in *Moore v. Dempsey*, p. 2.

"like popcorn popping": *Ed Ware et al. v. State of Arkansas*, p. 58.

"bullets just kept . . .": Ibid, p. 72.

"Negro plot . . .": McWhirter, p. 217.

"They were shooting . . .": Frank Moore quoted in Wells-Barnett, p. 21.

"Elaine Insurrection": *Helena World*, Oct. 3, 1919.

"To the Negroes. . ." and "as if nothing . . ." and "STOP TALKING . . .": Committee of Seven statement, October 7, 1919.

CHAPTER 2

"His word was . . ." and "a man of the . . .": Dillard interview with Will Sheppard, April 15, 1971.

"Justice!" and "All I ask . . .": Ovington, *Portraits*, p. 92.

"the fever": Whitaker, p. 16.

"that one scarcely . . ." Ovington, *Portraits*, p. 98.

"picking cotton . . .": Smiddy affidavit, *Moore v. Dempsey*, p. 95.

"a large number of . . .": Scipio Jones in *Moore v. Dempsey*, p. 35

"the minds of . . .": *Ed Ware et al. v. the State of Arkansas*, p. 141.

"was given to . . .": "Inward Facts About Negro Insurrection," Committee of Seven, Oct. 7, 1919.

CHAPTER 3

"Old Sparky": Arkansas Department of Corrections.

"solemn promise": American Legion Post 41 resolution, Oct. 19, 1920.

"dead, dead, dead": *Moore v. Dempsey*, p. 35.

"I went in the . . ." and "I had eight . . .": Wells-Barnett, p. 19.

"whipped nearly . . .": Frank Moore quoted in Wells-Barnett, p. 21.

"I have the scars . . .": Ibid, p. 18.

"So terror-inspiring . . ." and "that not a word . . .": *Ed Ware et al. v. the State of Arkansas*, p. 140.

"to make us lie": John Martin and Alfred Banks quoted in Wells-Barnett, p. 18.

"definite idea . . .": Moore v. Dempsey, p. 37.

"under the Constitution . . .": Ibid., p. 77.

"put in an electric chair . . .": Wells-Barnett, p. 22.

CHAPTER 4

"a northern organization . . .": Mary White Ovington quoted in McWhirter, p. 228.

"heart and center . . .": Monroe Work quoted in Stockley, p. 162.

"a race riot" and "an uprising": Jones, *The Crisis*,
    December 1921, p. 73.
"no friends at all": Ed Ware, "I Stand and Wring My Hands
    and Cry," quoted in Wells-Barnett, p. 4.
"would move any . . .": James Weldon Johnson letter to
    Walter White, August 3, 1923 (Waskow papers).
"With my enemies . . .": Ed Ware, "I Stand and Wring My
    Hands and Cry," quoted in Wells-Barnett, p. 4.
"the possible killing . . .": Whitaker, p. 222.

CHAPTER 5

"We must win. . . .": Scipio Jones letter to Walter White,
    March 25, 1921.
"an intense prejudice . . .": *Ed Ware et al. v. the State of
    Arkansas*, p. 5.
"talesmen": Ibid., p. 13.
"A great many . . ." and "qualifications being . . .": Ibid., p. 2.
"a civil one . . .": Ibid., p. 138.
"everybody shot": Ibid., p. 17.
"no bullet holes . . .": Ibid., p. 29.
"If you don't believe . . .": Ibid., p. 49.
"if it was not . . .": Ibid., p. 141.
"The trouble about it . . .": Ibid.
"killing our own men": Joseph Fox and Albert Giles quoted in
    Wells-Barnett, p. 17.
"Is it not striking . . .": *Ed Ware et al. v. the State of Arkansas*,
    p. 141.

CHAPTER 6

"We, the jury . . .": *Ed Ware et al. v. the State of Arkansas*,
    pp. 41, 63, 77, 101, 124.
"We and our attorneys . . ." and "prejudice was left . . .":
    Cortner, p. 93.
"absolute justice": Stockley, p. 174.

"on the very hour": Ovington, *Portraits,* p. 99.

"All we can do . . .": Cortner, p. 93.

"Last Hope Gone . . .": *Arkansas Gazette,* Nov. 30, 1920, in Whitaker, p. 234.

"still insisting . . .": Cortner, p. 100.

"Let the courts . . .": *Arkansas Democrat,* Nov. 17, 1920, in Whitaker, p. 235.

"Law abiding citizens . . .": Cortner, p. 101.

"I am pretty sure . . ." and "I am selfish enough . . .": Scipio Jones letter to Walter White, Dec. 15, 1920, quoted in Whitaker, p. 235.

CHAPTER 7

"bull-dog tenacity": *Arkansas Survey,* January 17, 1925, quoted in Dillard.

"Any place is . . .": Whitaker, p. 239.

"solemn promise": American Legion Post 41 resolution, Oct. 19, 1920.

"I don't know where . . ." Scipio Jones letter to Walter White, March 25, 1921, quoted in Whitaker, p. 237.

"These men should not . . .": Ibid.

"there would not . . .": John Miller letter to Gov. Thomas C. McRae, June 6, 1921. (Waskow papers).

"no more promises . . .": Whitaker, p. 244.

"Scipio Jones won't . . .": Ovington, *Walls,* p. 160.

CHAPTER 8

"No imminent danger . . .": Whitaker, p. 250.

"What a counsel . . .": Stockley, p. 190.

"to cut through . . ." Ibid., p. 189.

"dominated by a mob": Whitaker, p. 255.

"a corrective process": Ibid.

CHAPTER 9

"Benches were turned . . .": Smiddy affidavit, *Moore v. Dempsey*, p. 92.

"So far as I know . . .": TK Jones affidavit, *Moore v. Dempsey*, pp. 89-90.

"The feeling against them . . .": *Moore v. Dempsey* pp. 123–124.

"began to make . . .": Ibid, p. 169.

"the colored lawyer . . .": Cortner, 133.

"assumed and exercised . . ." and "but as part . . .": *Moore v. Dempsey*, p. 3.

"the verdict of . . .": Ibid., p. 5-6.

"with the facts stated . . .": Whitaker, p. 265.

"The greatest case . . .": *The Crisis*, January 19, 1922, p. 117.

CHAPTER 10

"one of the . . .": Whitaker, p. 270.

"bitterness beyond . . .": Jones, *The Crisis*, December 1921, p. 75.

"the judgment against . . ." Ibid., p. 76.

"it would be . . .": Whitaker, p. 278.

"a splendid . . .": Cortner, p. 146.

"Don't expect to be . . ." and "Depending on . . .": Whitaker, p. 282.

"You demurred . . .": Ibid., p. 284.

"does not seem . . .": CALS *Encyclopedia of Arkansas History & Culture*.

CHAPTER 11

"ready for trial . . .": attributed to Stockley, p. 218.

"Please Sir . . ." and "Walk on the ground . . .": Ed Ware letter to Scipio Jones, February 12, 1923. (Waskow papers).

"Justice delayed . . .": Stockley, p. 220.

"mighty fine": Cortner, p. 164.

"You're free to go!": attributed to Whitaker, p. 297.

"You never heard . . .": Whitaker, p. 298.

CHAPTER 12

"They have simply . . .": *Arkansas Gazette*, "The Breakdown of the Law in the Elaine Cases" (Waskow papers).

"I did what I . . .": Cortner, p. 170.

"They want to get . . .": Ibid., p. 170.

"forced to leave . . .": Ibid., p. 169.

"strictly confidential": Ibid., p. 175.

"Do you think . . .": Scipio Jones letter to Walter White, April 2, 1923. (Waskow papers).

"the very great moral . . ."; Herbert K. Stockton letter to Robert W. Bagnall, April 18, 1923 (Waskow papers).

"Even if we lost . . .": James Weldon Johnson letter to Walter White, August 3, 1923. (Waskow papers).

"full and complete . . .": Scipio Jones letter to Walter White, Nov. 3, 1923, quoted in Whitaker, p. 301.

"it would be fair . . .": Ibid.

"I hesitate to . . .": Ibid.

"not receive clemency": Whitaker, p. 304.

CHAPTER 13

"financial wreck": Whitaker, p. 271.

"Anticipate favorable . . .": Stockley, p. 223.

"cauldron of hate": *Arkansas Survey*, January 17, 1925, quoted in Dillard.

"All hail . . .": Ibid.

EPILOGUE

"There are no . . .": Richardson, p. 459.

"rendered a service . . .": Cortner, p. 183.

"believed their lives . . ." and "Very few . . .": University of Arkansas at Little Rock statement, November 8, 2018.

"We believe the missing . . .": Ibid.

"life and death . . .": Scipio Jones letter to Walter White, March 25, 1921, quoted in Whitaker, p. 237.

Soldiers from Camp Pike set up tents in downtown Elaine after the massacre.

Scipio's house in Little Rock is listed on the National Register of Historic Places. The home was abandoned when this photo was taken in 2018.

INDEX

Page numbers in **boldface** indicate photographs and/or captions.

135

PICTURE CREDITS

AP Images, photographer Danny Johnston, 116

Arkansas Department of Corrections, 33, 63

Arkansas State Archives, 49

Butler Center for Arkansas Studies, Central Arkansas Library System, 20, 30–31, 67, 83, 86, 90, 93, 102, 110 (top and bottom)

Charles Hillman Brough Papers, Arkansas State Archives, 12, 13, 14, 16–17 (top), 29, 35, 58, 73, 133

Courtesy of the Senator John Heinz History Center, 104 (top)

Department of Special Collections and University Archives, W. E. B. Du Bois Library, University of Massachusetts, Amherst, 8 (left)

Encyclopedia of Arkansas History & Culture, 16 (bottom)

©**Kuchin Victor/Shutterstock.com,** 1, 3

Library of Congress, 68 (top), 78 (bottom); **Prints and Photographs Division, Visual Materials from the NAACP Records,** LC-DIG-ppmsca-09705: 40; LC-DIG-ppmsca-38685: 104 (bottom); **Prints and Photographs Division, George Grantham Bain Collection:** 78 (top), 100; **Prints and Photographs Division, Harris & Ewing Collection:** 84

Sandra Neil Wallace, 117, 134

U.S. Farm Security Administration, Office of War Information Photograph Collection (Library of Congress): photographer Ben Shahn, 8 (top), 8 (bottom), 27, 28, 52, 108, 118, 126, 140; photographer Russell Lee, 68 (bottom); photographer Dorothea Lange, 74–75

U.S. National Archives and Records Administration, 11, 18

University of Chicago Photographic Archive, Special Collections Research Center, University of Chicago Library (Webb Studio), 38

University of Louisville, 43 (top and bottom)

ABOUT THE AUTHORS

Investigative journalists **Sandra Neil Wallace** and **Rich Wallace** are award-winning writers of nonfiction titles including *First Generation: 36 Trailblazing Immigrants and Refugees Who Make America Great* and *Blood Brother: Jonathan Daniels and His Sacrifice for Civil Rights*, which won the International Literacy Association's Social Justice Award. Sandra's picture-book biography *Between the Lines: How Ernie Barnes Went from the Football Field to the Art Gallery* earned the Orbis Pictus Award for Outstanding Nonfiction. The authors' other recent books have won the Paterson Prize, the California Reading Association's Eureka Gold Award, and the Parents' Choice Gold Award and have been named to many "best books" lists such as the ALA-ALSC Notable Children's Books. Sandra and Rich live in Keene, New Hampshire. Visit them at sandraneilwallace.com and richwallacebooks.com

Black farmers in the Arkansas Delta who organized for economic power planted the seed for future generations to advocate for pay equity.

OTHER CALKINS CREEK TITLES FROM SANDRA NEIL WALLACE AND RICH WALLACE

Babe Conquers the World: The Legendary Life of Babe Didrikson Zaharias
ALA-YALSA Quick Pick for Reluctant Readers
New Hampshire Literary Award, Outstanding Work of Nonfiction runner-up

Blood Brother: Jonathan Daniels and His Sacrifice for Civil Rights (available only as ebook)
ALA-ALSC Notable Children's Book
International Literacy Association Social Justice Literature Award
Booklist Editors' Choice
NCSS CBC Notable Social Studies Trade Book for Young People
Parents' Choice Gold Award
Chicago Public Library Best of the Best Books
Paterson Prize for Books for Young People
YALSA Award for Excellence in Nonfiction for Young Adults, official nominee

Bound by Ice: A True North Pole Survival Story
Kirkus Reviews Best Children's Book
NCSS CBC Notable Social Studies Trade Book for Young People
New Hampshire Literary Award, Middle-Grade Young Adult winner
Bank Street College Best Children's Book of the Year
California Reading Association, Eureka! Nonfiction Children's Gold Award

The Teachers March!: How Selma's Teachers Changed History
(Fall 2020)
Booklist, Kirkus Reviews, and *Publishers Weekly*, starred reviews